Poems of
Mao Tse-tung

Poems of Mao Tse-tung

TRANSLATION, INTRODUCTION, AND NOTES BY

Hua-ling Nieh Engle
and
Paul Engle

A DELTA BOOK

A DELTA BOOK
Published by
DELL PUBLISHING CO., INC.
1 Dag Hammarskjold Plaza
New York, New York 10017

Delta ® TM 755118, Dell Publishing Co., Inc.
Reprinted by arrangement with
Simon and Schuster, Inc.
New York, New York 10020
Printed in the United States of America
First Delta printing—October 1973

The authors gratefully acknowledge
permission to reprint material from
China Awake by Robert Payne, Copyright 1947
by Robert Payne, published by Dodd, Mead & Co.

Acknowledgments

Of many books consulted for background information, Edgar Snow's *Red Star Over China* and Robert Payne's *Mao Tse-tung* we found indispensable, and we urge that they be read.

Wan Kin Lau, from Hong Kong, helped with translations of some materials and library research.

Ming-sun Poon, Far Eastern Library, University of Chicago, was very helpful in copying and sending books and articles.

Mrs. Sharon Rohner, our secretary at the University of Iowa, prepared the manuscript with speed, accuracy, and extra hours.

We thank them for their devoted help.

We wish, too, to thank the Louis W. and Maud Hill Family Foundation of St. Paul, Minnesota, for their contribution and their belief in the importance of translating.

The University of Iowa and its School of Letters have been generous, as always, in their tradition of friendliness to literature and translation.

Contents

Introduction

It is proper that the ruler of the country with the most people in the world should sell more copies of his book of poems than any poet in history. It is probably true that the fifty-seven million copies said to have been sold of the poems of Mao Tse-tung may well equal the number of all volumes of poetry by all poets writing in English from the beginning of time.

Other leaders of nations have practiced an art. Kings have played the flute; presidents have painted on Sunday or played waltzes on the piano. When the British Army was besieging the Rommel line in the North African desert, not moving ahead and thus with plenty of time, General Lord Wavell held a poetry contest. Henry the Eighth played music when he was not playing other games. But these were not commitments of the life. They were diversions to release the tensions of power.

Mao's poetry is an intense political-military autobiography. He put his own life in danger many times during the Communist-Nationalist fighting in the Kiangsi and Hunan provinces (southeastern China) during the late twenties and early thirties. On the Long March he almost died three times. Often he would write a poem about a battle not long after it took place ("Chingkang Mountain," 1928 and "Fighting Against the 'First Siege,'" 1931 are examples). Several poems were written on the Long March, in the middle of that turbulent and deadly walk, when surely the minds of few were on poetry ("Lou Mountain Pass," 1935 and "The Long March," October, 1935).

Every poem has its immediate or distant connection with

actual events in Mao's share of recent Chinese history. There are no purely "private" poems concerned with his own personal life. Even when he mentions, in a rare moment of reference to one of his marriages, the name of his first wife, he has no ordinary emotional language. He calls her his "tough willow," because she refused to repudiate him and the Communist party and was executed by the Nationalists in Changsha. She was the daughter of Mao's favorite teacher at college, bore him children, was apparently so devoted to him and to the cause for which they both worked that she preferred death to making a statement which would have saved her life. ("Reply to Li Shu-yi," 1957—she had discovered that her husband had been killed by the Nationalists and had sent Mao a poem about him. In the traditional Chinese way, Mao replies with his own poem.) One of the two sons Yang bore was killed fighting in Korea. Not one word in the poem is personal or tender. All celebrate the revolutionary cause. Yang is remembered not as woman and wife, but as fighter.

This is true of all Mao's poems. Whatever the apparent subject, whatever the title, no matter how much countryside is described (Mao regularly praises the Chinese landscape more than he does individuals, save for the occasional use of "hero"), the one concern is always the Communist cause. At the same time that Yang was arrested in Changsha, Mao's sister Tse-hung was also arrested and executed. Not one word of regret in any poem, no family sentiment. In a paragraph from his indispensable book *Red Star Over China*, which should be read in conjunction with this volume, Edgar Snow writes of Mao:

He obviously considered the individual of very little importance. Like other Reds I met he tended to talk only about committees, organizations, armies, resolutions, battles, tactics, 'measures,' and so on, and seldom of personal experience. . . . I found repeatedly that the Communist would be able to tell everything that had happened in his early youth, but once he had become identified with the Red Army he lost himself somewhere, and without repeated questioning one could hear nothing about *him*, but only stories of the Army, or the Soviets, or the

Party—capitalized. These men could talk indefinitely about dates and circumstances of battles, and movements to and from a thousand unheard-of places, but those events seemed to have had significance for them only collectively, not because they as individuals had made history there, and behind it the whole organic force of an ideology for which they were fighting.

Can poetry be written out of such attitudes? Mao has done it. His solution was to write in precise classical forms, in which the length of each line, the number of syllables, and the sequence of rime had been rigidly set many hundreds of years ago. The *tzu* and *shih* had been intricately worked out, especially in the T'ang Dynasty (618-906 A.D.), the former having a tune in it, long since lost. In these intricate and conventional forms, Mao expressed his revolutionary ideas, and yet not with the dullness of most radical verse. It may be that the demands of the form saved his poetry from the doggerel into which so much fervent, even deeply felt, poetry of revolt so often falls. The form is always scrupulously maintained, and the theme is always strongly revolutionary. In Mao, the politics and the poetry are like bands of muscle wrapped around each other: when one is flexed, the other moves.

Mao has been accused by Soviet critics of preferring "revolutionary romanticism" to "socialist realism." It may be that this doctrinaire distinction reveals why Mao is able to create imaginative poetry out of what otherwise could be mere slogans. In one of his "Talks at the Yenan Forum," where in 1942 he laid down his principles of aesthetic practise, Mao said: "Although man's social life is the only source of literature and art and is incomparably livelier and richer in content, the people are not satisfied with life alone and demand literature and art as well. Why? Because, while both are beautiful, life as reflected in works of literature and art can and ought to be on a higher plane, more intense, more concentrated, more typical, nearer the ideal, and therefore more universal than everyday life."

Mao is at all times clearly aware of his own experience and its relevance to others. Mao considered the "cultural front," from the start, to be as important as military operations. In a time of social disorder and war, literature has a special importance. Chiang Kai-shek tended to think of the war against the Communists in essentially military terms, but Mao always, even in the darkest times of defeat and flight, urged the recognition of the power of the arts to shape men's minds, and it was that shaping, rather than military victories, which he felt in the long run was the Communist party's firmest strength. At Yenan, he indulged in one of his rare self-revelations:

If you want the masses to understand you, if you want to be one with the masses, you must make up your mind to undergo a long and even painful process of tempering. Here I might mention the experience of how my own feelings changed. I began life as a student and at school acquired the ways of a student; I then used to feel it undignified to do even a little manual labor, such as carrying my own luggage in the presence of my fellow students, who were incapable of carrying anything, either on their shoulders or in their hands. At that time I felt that intellectuals were the only clean people in the world, while in comparison workers and peasants were dirty. I did not mind wearing the clothes of other intellectuals, believing them clean, but I would not put on clothes belonging to a worker or peasant, believing them dirty. But after I became a revolution-ary and lived with workers and peasants and with soldiers of the revolutionary army, I gradually came to know them well, and they gradually came to know me well too. . . . I came to feel that compared with the workers and peasants the unre-molded intellectuals were not clean and that, in the last analysis, the workers and peasants were the cleanest people and, even though their hands were soiled and their feet smeared with cow-dung, they were really cleaner than the bourgeois and petty-bourgeois intellectuals.

In the same talk, Mao speaks of "comrades" who argue that everything ought to start from "love." "Now as for love, in a class society there can be only class love; but these comrades are seeking a love transcending classes, love in the abstract and also freedom in the abstract, truth in the abstract, human nature in the abstract, etc." It is right for artists and writers to study literary and artistic creation, but they must also study society. They must learn the rich and lively language of the people.

There is no easy definition of Mao's attitude to poetry, for his theory seems usually opposed to his own practise. In one of the Yenan talks he said, "There is in fact no such thing as art for art's sake, art that stands above classes or art that is detached from or independent of politics." Art must serve the revolution, it must appeal to the "masses." Yet it is doubtful that Mao's own vocabulary in his poems, or the forms in which they are cast, would be wholly intelligible to the masses.

One of Mao's problems may well be that he grew up in a rigid society and has no concept of any condition as fluid as American society. His remark that "The bourgeoisie always shuts out proletarian literature and art, however great their artistic merit" is certainly repudiated by the popularity among all manner of people in the U.S.A. of writings by minorities and the impoverished. Yet Mao later insists that "Works of art which lack artistic quality have no force, however progressive they are politically. Therefore, we oppose both the tendency to produce works of art with a wrong political viewpoint and the tendency towards the 'poster and slogan style' which is correct in political viewpoint but lacking in artistic power." He also ridicules "veiled and roundabout expressions, which are hard for the people to understand." By Western standards, there are many veiled and roundabout expressions in Mao's poetry, and some of those are the most effective.

It is the unity of politics and art which Mao says is desirable, the unity of content and form. "The unity of revolutionary political content and the highest possible perfection of artistic form" is the phrase of Mao's which best describes his own work. Every poem is perfected in its traditional form, and every poem makes a revolutionary assertion. He has combined a strong poetic imagination with a strong practical (and military) mind. It is characteristic of Mao that when he set down his famous principles of guerrilla warfare he not only carried them out in daily fighting with the Nationalist armies trying to encircle and destroy the much smaller Communist forces in Kiangsi Province in the late twenties, he also put them into terse rimed couplets:

> Enemy advance, we run away.
> Enemy stop, we delay.
> Enemy tired, we annoy.
> Enemy retreat, we destroy.

What other commander in history has put his strategy into verse while actively fighting?

Mao quotes with approval a couplet from the writer Lu Hsun in which he says that he coolly defies "a thousand pointing fingers" and, with bowed head like a willing ox, serves the people. This demonstrates his idea of political fervor and excellence of form. When Mao wrote a poem about revisiting his native village, Shaoshan, in Hunan Province, south China, he does not recall its famous hot peppers, which he loved to eat, nor his harsh, semi-illiterate father, nor his kind, illiterate, devoutly Buddhist mother (she taught him to sing Buddhist hymns as a child!), nor the fields to which he had carried manure, but the peasant spears he had seen raised in revolt. The exact phrase might be—revolutionary-romantic-realistic wine, poured into the old but beautiful bottles of classical form.

It would seem that Mao has written poetry all of his life. The first poem in this book, "Changsha," is dated 1925, when Mao was thirty-two years old. The last is dated 1965, when he was seventy-two years old. Thus, forty years of the most intense physical, military, and political activity covered the period of his known poetry. No one could have achieved the control of ancient form in "Changsha" if it had been his first poem. He must have written poems in his youth. Robert Payne says that Mao published a collection of his poems at Yenan called *Wind Sand Poems*. We could not get it. Poems are included there which do not appear in the later collections. Payne insists that Mao's friends said that he wrote verse even as a boy. In Yenan, Payne reports, during meetings of the "Soviet" government, Mao wrote poems as other men did doodles on paper and then threw them on the floor; members of the meeting rushed to pick them up, so that there may be Mao poems still unpublished as well as wholly unknown.

Mao's attitude toward his poetry is humble and, indeed, self-deprecating. His letter to the editors of the magazine, *Poetry*, in answer to their request to print some of his poems, is very revealing:

Comrade Ko-chia and other Comrades:

I received your letter a long time ago. Sorry for delay in replying. You asked me to send you such of my poems in the old forms as I can remember. I have copied them on other sheets of paper, along with the eight poems you sent me, totalling eighteen poems. I send them all to you. Deal with them as you think fit.

These poems I have never been willing to publish because they are in old forms. I was afraid the wrong kind of poetry would be circulated and harm the young. Also, they are not poetic enough, nor in any way distinguished. Since you think they can be published, and you will also correct the wrong words in some of the circulated poems which others have wrongly copied, then I let you do as you wish.

The magazine *Poetry* has appeared. Good. I hope it will grow and develop. Of course, the main thing should be poetry in new forms. Poems may sometimes be written in the old forms, but they should not be encouraged among the young, because the old forms restrict thought and are hard to learn. These words are only for your reference.

Salutations from the Comrade,
MAO TSE-TUNG
January 12, 1957

Even with this disparagement of his own writing and of his use of the old forms, Mao went right on producing new poems—his private reactions to public events, such as building an immense bridge or halting an epidemic in one part of China. No poem is "personal" in the Western meaning of an individual putting into moving language an emotional moment in his life. Mao the man is in the poem, but only as the transmuter of incidents in the struggle for control of China and the actions which were taken once that power had been achieved.

Every poem has its ultimate motivation and subject matter in the Communist movement: places where battles were fought with the Nationalists; landscapes where the Red Army fled, as on the Long March; mountains, swamps, rivers, bridges involved in the party's defeats and triumphs. Great episodes which would have produced a chapter of another leader's memoirs produced in Mao a poem. He poured his personal feelings into the public history. In a sense, the party was his life. Although he married three times (not including a traditional ceremony as a boy when he was married to a little girl with whom he never lived), his profoundest relationship was with the party. All his waking hours when he was building an organization to take over China went to that one purpose; sleep was a way of gaining more strength for the next day's efforts.

There was always a tradition in China that heads of state wrote poetry. Mao produced classical verse before he produced Communist theory. Suppose Marx had written sonnets in the Italian form, instead of that opaque prose! The Chinese used to quote the thoughts of Confucius. Now they quote the thoughts of Mao. In this sense, Mao is an extension of old Chinese habits, but changed to a revolutionary purpose.

When the poems mentioned by Mao in his letter to the editors of *Poetry* were published, they were reprinted all over China: in all the daily newspapers from the largest, *People's Daily*, to small local papers on the frontiers, and in literary, economic, political, and scientific periodicals. The annual reference book on China, *People's Handbook*, the standard work on developments in China, carried the poems in 1958. The poems were published that same year in English translation by the Foreign Languages Press in Peking.

It is relevant to note that Mao used images in the manner of poetry even while using prose. Perhaps his most famous remark describes the revolutionary as a fish swimming in the sea of the people. Of the enemy he said that he is bread which can satisfy "our hunger." His images come largely out of his tough peasant background: "Take a bucket of water, for instance; where is it to be raised from if not from the ground? From mid-air? From what basis, then, are literature and art to be raised?" The basis to which he refers is, of course, not the intellectual or the bourgeoisie but the familiar worker-peasant-soldier combination. These latter are often uneducated, and for them the primary need is not "more flowers on the brocade," but "coal in snowy weather." Mao once said that democracy is like rice, "which we now get from Hankow—it takes time and it costs money and there are people who try to intercept it."

The man himself was described in a shrewd and lively manner by Robert Payne in his book *China Awake*, published in 1947. Payne saw much of Mao at Yenan.

Photographs are unfaithful and give no impression of the man with the long streaming blue-black hair, the round silver-rimmed spectacles, the fine cheek-bones, the pursed, almost feminine lips and the air of a college professor. Usually, you see him in photographs wearing a cloth cap, and you notice the round peasant face and the small nose and the heavy eyes —but the moment the cap is taken off the peasant disappears. It is true that he hardly ever remains the same for more than a few minutes on end, so that one moment he giggles like a boy, and the next moment the soft voice takes on depth and authority and a quite extraordinary resonance. He is fifty-three and looks thirty. You will see him any day on any campus in England or America.

Partly, of course, it is the fault of the legend. If you remember the Long March, if you remember Edgar Snow's famous story of Mao Tse-tung undoing his trousers and scrabbling for fleas, or taking off his trousers altogether when he entered Lin Piao's cave on a sweltering hot day and gazing at a map on the wall, then you will be perfectly satisfied to regard him as part military genius, part peasant leader and part barbarian. . . . Mao has matured and taken on a deeper gravity of manner, but he was obviously never the barbarian. Agnes Smedley describes how she was shocked by his femininity. It is perfectly true that there is a streak of femininity in him, as there is in all Chinese scholars to the extent that their gestures are graceful, they speak in carefully modulated soft voices and sing their poems falsetto. . . . Ultimately a man is what he is without his cap. Remove the cap, and Mao Tse-tung gives all the appearance of a scholar. . . . The course of study he has set himself is the revolution of China. . . .

[Mao steadily refused to talk about himself or his poetry, preferring to reminisce about those with him on the Long March, as in the following passage from Payne, quoting Mao at an evening party.] "It was extraordinary. Chu Teh [Mao's friend and leading general—TRANSLATORS] had the courage to go through the grasslands *twice*. It was pretty dangerous to go through it once, but twice—" The legend of the Long March returned; he had no desire to side-track it, and answered the professors' questions gravely. . . . The Communists were old men now. The Long March was still the legend around which their lives revolved. . . . He [Mao—TRANSLATORS] spoke of the grasslands again. "We killed our oxen and horses for meat, and carried them on our few remaining baggage animals, and then in the end we ate the baggage animals and carried the meat ourselves. It was desperately hard, and the best fighters we ever had to face were the aboriginal tribes—the Miaos, the Fans, the Mis and the Huans. We learnt from them more than we learnt from anyone else. . . ."

He looked grim now. The line of the mouth became hard and determined, the voice deeper, the gestures far more restrained. But I hadn't come to talk about politics—I wanted to find more of his poems and translate them. He grinned again: "They're really very bad—terribly bad. I just write poetry to waste time."

It was useless, whatever you said about his poetry, he had one final, absolute answer—it was shockingly bad, and he would be ashamed to have it seen. It was nonsense, but the kind of nonsense that gave him pleasure, for he giggled again, knowing only too well that the poetry was good. He had written a poem called *The Snow* which had become famous all over China. "I gave it to my friend, urging him not to let anyone see it, but he published it without my permission."

There are definite recurring themes in Mao's poetry. Time and again he uses the word "will," as at the end of

"Chingkang Mountain" (1965, on the occasion of revisiting the place of the Red Army's 1928 hideout), where he says that nothing in this world is difficult if you have the will to keep climbing. In his poem on Shaoshan he writes that only because so many sacrificed themselves did "our" wills become strong. Mao was once arrested and escaped. He was expelled from the office he held in the party. He is one of the least discourageable and most strongly willed men in history. By sufficient will, a few people can conquer an immense nation—and write poetry while doing it, if they have the will to power to gain that repose in the midst of action which is necessary for writing.

Another implied theme is that the Communist party and Mao are the culmination of Chinese history. He cites ancient emperors in some poems, but complains that they were not cultured enough. Now (under the Communists) the old ways which led to hunger, oppression, illiteracy, foreign interference, and Chinese humiliation have been destroyed. The new system will stop all those flaws and, in addition, has given the Chinese a pride in themselves. The foreign concessions, foreign gunboats up the mainland rivers, were a great affront to many, especially the university students, and Mao's opposition to them was one reason his struggle was popular with so many of the young.

Everywhere in the poems there is an intense feeling for the landscape of China. Mao is concerned not only with *what* is happening but with the fields, mountains, rivers where it is happening. "Snow" especially celebrates the look of the country: "Mountains, silver snakes dancing;/ plateaus, wax-white elephants running. . . . Some fine day you will see the land/dressed in red, wrapped with white,/ flirting, enchanting."

Another theme to which Mao returns several times is the need for change, the capacity to change not only the natural forces of China (bridging rivers, conquering diseases) but to change human nature itself, to which end the social and political system must be changed. Here again, a tough enough will can make all this possible. "Who controls this rise and fall?" Mao asks. One might suggest that he has himself in mind, and his party, as the instrument of change.

Still another way in which Mao has joined traditional Chinese manners with the contemporary world is in his exchanges of poems with friends. Several people wrote poems to him and he replied in verse. Mrs. Li Shu-yi wrote him about her husband being killed by the Nationalists and Mao wrote a poem back about his own wife being killed by them. The poem from which President Nixon quoted in Peking was "Reply to Comrade Kuo Mo-jo," written in 1963 in answer to Kuo's poem. (Kuo was an old friend of Mao and has held many offices in the government.)

All of the poems in this volume appear in the official collected edition published in Peking, except for "Chingkang Mountain," 1965. This was published in the Hong Kong magazine *Ming Pao*, where Hua-ling Nieh's novel is currently being serialized. In glancing through the magazine, she found this previously unknown poem and we promptly translated it, pleased to find that it fit the same pattern as the earlier poems.

Just as Mao almost never uses the pronoun "I," neither does he express much bitterness. In "Chingkang Mountain," 1965, at the scene of great suffering and almost constant attack, there is no hate, no gloating over triumph, only mention of laughter and talk and determination.

At the end of the Long March, Mao wrote "Kunlun," about one mountain in that great range coming east out of Tibet and pushing deep into China. With the Red Army, he had crossed a portion of that range, in severe wind, snow, and cold where many died. Decimated, shattered, hungry, the remnants, hardly a fifth of the original number, struggled into Yenan. Yet Mao ignores all that suffering in his poem, that long flight, and has only a remarkable sense of the world with which to conclude. It must have taken great detachment and good will to have expressed these lines at such a time. He says to the mountain that it is too high, it has too much snow:

Leaning against the sky,
could I draw a sword
and cut you into three pieces?
Give one piece to Europe,
send one piece to America,
return one piece to Asia,
a world in peace,
sharing together your heat and cold.

Each poem is a window into the character of Mao, an insight into how he blends the most remote names in Chinese history with the most urgent situation in the present. There is probably no other example of the leader of a revolution, and of a vast nation, who concentrated his profoundest sense of what was happening in his country in carefully made poems.

Those tight classical forms may have been necessary to control the turbulent events about which Mao was writing, and the turbulence in his own mind.

A Note on Translation

A hundred years from now, unless everyone is speaking Chinese and nothing needs to be translated, critics will be attacking translators.

All translation is impossible, and all possible translation must be done. A long time ago theologians believed that "translation" meant the immediate removal to heaven of a body without intervening death, the intact and beautiful body. But anyone who ever translates knows that the body never comes across perfect and pure. A literal, word-by-word translation is hardly a shadow of the original, and an "imitation," in which the poet converts a text from another language (which he may not know) to a mirror image of his own style, is a way of possessing a poem which his imagination did not create.

All translation is literally impossible, especially if it is literal. Yet marvelous things have been done. The world we live in is the result of translation, the spread of religions and trade being impossible without it. One of the majestic intellectual acts of the human race was surely the transmuting of the Buddhist texts from Sanskrit, with its long polysyllabic words, into Chinese, with its one-word characters.

With all of its dangers and disasters, translation is one of the most urgent and most miraculous human actions.

The problems of translating from Chinese are of a far higher range of difficulty than the problems of translating from Western languages into English. The whole visual effect is different, but above all the auditory effects cannot be in any way reproduced. The four tones of each character contribute much to the musicality of Chinese poetry. They have no equivalents in English.

The Chinese language offers far more ambiguity of meaning than English, because it does not use tenses of verbs (past, present, future are the same, which suggests a sense of living in eternity), cases, or moods. Often the phrase "ten thousand" will be used when only "a great many" is intended. This has, however, the advantage of allowing poetry to be impersonal, universal, timeless.

Chinese pronounce the question mark (*ma?*) and the exclamation point (*ba!*)—a very simple and enriching quality, making the language more dramatic.

Robert Payne has an insightful passage about this problem. In *China Awake*, he writes:

We were talking about translations from Chinese, and the hideous difficulties that arise in transferring a language of clear-cut ideograms into the alphabetical monstrosities we have in the West. . . . a Chinese character never means exactly the same as an English word. Its associations, its music, its color, its sound, its place in a sentence, the peculiar effect of shadowing, by which one word throws its accent and shape on another, all these are different. . . .

Foreign translations of Chinese poetry are full of mistakes. Even the translations of great sinologues like Arthur Waley have errors. Florence Asycough's versions of Tu Fu, which she composed with Amy Lowell and with the assistance of a Chinese scholar, are sometimes incredibly muddle-headed. There is a translation of some of *The Three Hundred Poems of the T'ang Dynasty* by a curator of the British Museum which according to a Chinese scholar I know is almost childish in their simpleminded delight in making errors. But is this true? They have made mistakes certainly, because it is impossible for a western mind to realize all the associations implied in the Chinese. They have done their best. Too often they were not poets, and possessed little enough feeling for poetry. . . .

But there is one very great American poet, who knew as far as I know no Chinese at all, yet he is by far the best of all the translators of Chinese poetry. He made mistakes, but at least he gave the sense and the fiery spirit of the original. He writes cleanly, as we [the Chinese—TRANSLATORS] wrote cleanly. . . .

I assure you Pound's translations of Chinese give me more pleasure (and considerably more annoyance) than all the other translations put together.

Even the Chinese have trouble within their own language. Edgar Snow reports that their version of the word "soviet" was *Su Wei-ai*, and when a delegation of peasants came to meet the Red Army on the Long March, they welcomed "Mr. Soviet." He also says that a Fukien militarist once posted a notice offering a reward for the capture, dead or alive, of "Su Wei-ai," a fellow who had been doing a lot of damage to landlords and must be exterminated.

One example will indicate the difficulty in translating these poems. The last line of Mao's celebration of the taking of Nanking by the People's Liberation Army has been variously translated. One version in *Ten More Poems of Mao Tse-tung*, published by the Eastern Horizon Press, Hong Kong, says, "But in man's world seas change into mulberry fields." Stuart R. Schram translates the line, "The true way that governs the world of men is that of radical change."

Both versions have much of the intention of the original, yet it would be difficult to believe that they used the same line of Mao's poem.

As founders and directors of The International Writing Program at the University of Iowa, a community of gifted writers from all parts of the world, we have worked with people who wrote in all languages (few of which we knew), from all manner of political-social-historical backgrounds. We were accustomed to searching for a common humanity and a common imagination in texts very strange to us. Although none of them had been head of a state, we discovered that imaginative people can communicate with the fewest of words. We also found that, for translating into English, a skilled use of that language is quite as important as a knowledge of the original language. As Richard Howard, American translator from French, said, he translates well from French because he knows English so well.

All translations are a shadow cast by the live body of the original poem. The translator's job is to pump blood into the shadow. He never wholly brings it back to life, but he can make it breathe.

Arguments about individual phrasings can go on forever, and the two of us had them—late at night, tired, tears imminent. Our compromise has been to get as close to the Chinese meaning as we could while making as readable a version in English as we could. Some may fail less than others.

As translators, we were curious to see what sort of poems a head of state would write. As writers, we wondered whether Mao's poems would make attractive sense in English. As writers and translators, we knew clearly that often it is more difficult to transform another person's work into another language than to write one's own original text.

A Note on the Notes

Unlike most poetry in English, Mao's poems require a great deal of political, historical, mythological, and literary explanation. Thus, our notes should be read before the poems, as well as afterward. Without them, much of his verse would be in part unintelligible. We have provided such information as we could find to elucidate references in the poems to the Chinese past or to present actions.

Although Mao has argued that arts must draw their strength from the "masses," his own poems are written in classical characters which the average Chinese probably could not understand. This is consistent with his own admitted suspicion of his poetry as not healthy for the young. The question which needs now to be explored is: How admirable is the poetry of the young?

Hua-ling Nieh Engle
Paul Engle

Changsha

Autumn 1925

No city in China was as important for Mao Tse-tung as Changsha, the capital of Hunan Province in the south of the country below the immense Yangtze River. When Mao and his closest friend, Hsiao San, were at middle school in Hsianghsiang, they would walk the 30 miles to Changsha. In the early spring of 1911, Mao and Hsiao San entered the junior college and he first read the word "socialism" in a newspaper, a quiet event which would ultimately shake the twentieth century. (At school in Hsianghsiang he also first read about America. He told Snow: "I had first learned of America in an article which told of the American Revolution and contained a sentence like this, 'After eight years of difficult war, Washington won victory and built up his nation.'")

It was in Changsha that he heard about the April 27, 1911, Nationalist party uprising in Canton against the Manchu Dynasty in which 130 leaders of the movement attacked the government offices, forty-three being killed and twenty-seven captured and executed. They became famous all over China as "the seventy-two martyrs of the Yellow Flower Mound." It was in Changsha that Mao wrote political articles and put them up on walls as was done by young Communists years later in the Cultural Revolution. Mao also led "queue-chopping" expeditions against that sign of old tradition and claimed that he had cut ten queues. He had an argument with a law student who held that the body, skin, hair, and nails are heritages from one's parents and must not be destroyed.

A revolution broke out in Wuhan in October, 1911. A

short time later, the city of Changsha declared its independence. According to Payne, "Mao joined the regular army, in the hope that it would be sent immediately against Peking, but by the end of the year agreement between Sun Yat-sen [Leader of the Nationalist party revolt against the Manchu Dynasty; his ideas were far more liberal than those of the later Nationalist party and were expressed in his founding of the Republic of China.—TRANSLATORS] and Yuan Shih-kai, the warlord who had assumed power after the collapse of the Manchus, was in sight. Thirsting for a military career . . . Mao found himself a common soldier in Changsha on garrison duty. He was paid seven dollars a month, and his chief occupation was to be servant of the younger officers. . . . By the summer of 1912 he had left the Army and was living in poverty in a lodging-house."

Expecting to spend his life as a teacher, Mao entered the Teachers' Training College at Changsha and studied there for six years. (Payne says six years, Snow says five.) A typical comment of Mao's was (Snow): "There were many regulations in the new school and I agreed with very few of them." In Changsha, Mao also formed a discussion society of students—New People's Study Society—many of whom were later to be very important in Chinese affairs. They considered the times too serious to talk about women or personal affairs. Snow says that Mao and his friends walked out into the country long distances. If it rained, they took off their shirts and called it a rain bath. If the sun was hot, they took off their shirts and called it a sun bath. If the winds blew, they took off their shirts and called it a wind bath. Snow quotes Mao as describing himself in Changsha: "At this time my mind was a curious mixture of ideas of liberalism, democratic reformism, and utopian socialism. I had somewhat vague passions about 'nineteenth century democracy,' utopianism, and old-fashioned liberalism, and I was definitely anti-militarist and anti-imperialist. I had entered the normal school in 1912. I was graduated in 1918."

Changsha was later the scene of several armed engagements. It was taken over by the Communists and then by the Nationalist party and again by the Communists. It was the center for much of Mao's early revolutionary activity.

The Hsiang River, near which Mao was born, flows past Changsha on its way to the Yangtze. It is famous for its beauty. Orange Island is west of Changsha.

The school mates were members of the study circle who dedicated themselves to high ideals for the nation and the people. They opposed the efforts of Yuan Shih-kai to become emperor in September, 1915. The pamphlets and actions of the students stirred up the people against T'ang Hsiang-ming's repressive measures in favor of Yuan.

The line about the "thousand houses" probably refers to the warlords of Hunan Province, all of them enemies of liberal education.

CHANGSHA
Autumn 1925

Standing alone in the cold autumn,
where the Hsiang River flows north,
on the tip of Orange Island,
looking at thousands of hills,
red all over,
row after row of woods, all red,
the river is green to the bottom,
a hundred boats struggling,
eagles striking the sky,
fish gliding under the clear water.
All creatures fight for freedom
under the frosty sky.
Bewildered at empty space,
I ask the great, gray earth:
who controls the rise and fall?

Hundreds of friends used to come here.
Remember the old times—the years of fullness,
when we were students and young,
blooming and brilliant
with the young intellectuals'
emotional argument,
fist up, fist down,
fingers pointing
at river and mountain,
writings full of excitement,
lords of a thousand houses merely dung.
Remember still
how, in the middle of the stream,
we struck the water,
making waves which stopped
the running boats?

Yellow Crane Pavilion

Spring 1927

This is an ancient and legendary place on Yellow Crane Hill by the Yangtze west of Wuhan. It was said that a Taoist, Tsu-an, once flew past on a yellow crane going to join the immortals in the northwest of China (a curious anticipation of the Long March). In commemoration, a pavilion was erected and became a favorite visiting place of poets and scholars. It is mentioned in Peking opera and in novels. Li Po said farewell to a friend here. His contemporary, Ts'ui Hao, wrote a poem titled for the pavilion.

An ancient man flew away on the yellow crane.
Nothing remains here but the empty pavilion.
The yellow crane, once gone, never returns.
After a thousand years, white clouds still float alone.
In clear air over the river the trees of Han-yang are
    seen clearly,
and the fragrant grass lush on Parrot Island.
Where, in the setting sun, is my native place?
Mist and waves of the river make men sad.

The nine streams are the tributaries of the Yangtze. The iron line is the railroad. The two ways of travel, the ancient waterways and the modern iron track, are thus contrasted.

Turtle and Snake are names of mountains on opposite sides of the great Yangtze River, compressing it into turbulence. (Some commentators suggest that they represent anti-revolutionary forces squeezing the worker-peasant movement but only making it run deeper. They also hint that those who ride on the crane, which transported gods, become immortal, a reference to the revolutionaries who had died in the suppression of 1927 by the Nationalist party, which broke its agreement with the Communist party to work together against the warlords and the north.)

The whole poem is a fine example of Mao's cleverness in mingling mythology and politics in poetry, Marxist, in a Chinese form, as the politics may be.

There is a famous line of the Sung poet Su Tung-p'o, "To the moon on the river I drink a toast of wine." Mao has altered the line for his own contemporary purpose in toasting the dead comrades in the killings of the year. He is not content with taking the usual nostalgic way like the older poet, who wrote about the great river racing eastward.

YELLOW CRANE PAVILION
Spring 1927

Nine vast rivers rush through central China,
an iron line plunges north to south.
Rain, mist, gray, immense gray.
Turtle and Snake Mountains
block the great Yangtze River.

Where has the Yellow Crane flown?
Only the place for travelers remains.
Lifting the cup of wine to the pouring River,
my heart's tide surges wave-high.

Chingkang Mountain
Autumn 1928

Chingkang is a wide mountain area roughly 27 miles wide and 170 miles long. The peak on which Mao and the small Red Army group he brought there in October of 1927 after the failure of the "Autumn Harvest Uprising" in Hunan was named Ta Hsiao Wu Chin (Five Big-Little Wells, for the springs which flowed there). Mao had a thousand men and two hundred rifles. There were Buddhist temples all over the mountain which the Reds used as hospitals, offices, and dormitories. Clothes were hung on the age-darkened statues of the god. A printing press was set up, and newspapers were printed on the backs of Buddhist scrolls. Chingkang is on the border between the southern parts of Hunan and Kiangsi Provinces, the two regions in which Mao began his first operations as organizer and militant, armed enemy both of warlords and the Nationalist party. If there is one place which can be described as: "This is where it all began," it is Chingkang Mountain. Here the terms of guerrilla warfare were worked out in the most practical and painful way—by fighting and dying. Once Mao left the mountain in 1928, his struggle was never-ending until it culminated in the capture of the capital Nanking in April, 1949.

The troops of the Nationalist party assaulted the mountain many times, but the gorges, rough slopes, and forests made defense possible. The winter was bitter, food was scarce. Two bandits with armed peasants, Wang Tso and Yuan Wen-t'sai, threatened Mao's small band, but were persuaded to join instead. Conditions were rough, the soldiers inventing the slogan, "Down with capitalism; eat squash."

Communist politics are, if possible, more complicated than any in the world. Lyrical as Mao's verse is, the real basis of his poetry only reveals itself through a knowledge of the political scene. The terrible twentieth century (surely more men, women, and children have died violently than in any other period of the dismayed world's history) has produced a vast quantity of verse with political intent, most of it dreadful. In Mao the politics and the poetry are like bands of muscle wrapped around each other: when one is flexed, the other moves. Thus, "Chingkang Mountain" is a poem about power: the Nationalist party trying to destroy the Red force; the Reds not trying to expand, but merely to survive. And because they did survive, the guerrilla wars of the following years, culminating in the Long March, were possible.

Mao left the mountain in January, 1929, and began establishing soviets in southern Kiangsi.

Huang yang chieh is a place of winding and dangerous paths where several times the Nationalist party forces attacked and were repulsed. The noise of the cannon refers to a barrage fired to protect and conceal the retreat of the Chiang troops. Mao deliberately left Huang yang chieh unprotected to lure the Chiang troops into the ambush of his guerrilla soldiers.

CHINGKANG MOUNTAIN
Autumn 1928

Below the mountain, their flags flying,
High on the mountain, our bugles blowing:
A thousand circles of the enemy around us:
we still stand unmoved.

Defense is deadly, trench and wall,
the strongest fort is our will.
From Huang yang chieh cannon roar,
crying: the enemy runs away in the night.

War Between Chiang and the Kwangsi Clique

Autumn 1929

The warlords of Kwangsi Province (at the southern edge of China, bordering North Vietnam above Hanoi) were based at Hangkow. They fought Chiang because he was the leader of the Nationalist party.

The Golden Millet Dream is a T'ang Dynasty story about Lu Sheng, staying at an inn in Hantan, complaining about the bad luck in his life. A Taoist monk gave him a pillow and urged him to rest. While he slept, a meal of millet was being cooked on the stove. He had a dream in which all his ambitions were fulfilled: honors, power, riches, beautiful wife, sons and daughters marrying well, many grandchildren, living until over eighty. When he woke up, the meal of millet had still not been cooked. The point of Mao's lines is that the warlords will wake from their dream to find that their hopes have not been fulfilled.

In January, 1929, the Red General Chu Teh broke out of the Nationalist lines around Chingkang Mountain with the Red Fourth Army and crossed the Ting River, taking Lungyen and Shanghang in Fukien Province. This was close to the Communist center at Juichin, from which the Red Army set out on the Long March some five years later.

In classical Chinese literature, a golden vase was a symbol of a completely beautiful country. For Mao, it had been shattered by the warlords, and now he and the Red Army were putting back together such fragments of China as they could.

WAR BETWEEN CHIANG AND THE KWANGSI CLIQUE
Autumn 1929

Wind and clouds suddenly change,
Warlords begin war again,
raining on man's world all misery:
theirs is another Millet Dream in sleep.

Red flags leap over the Ting River,
running all the way to Lungyen and Shanghang.
Mending a fragment of the Golden Vase,
we are busy dividing farm and field.

Double Ninth Festival
October 1929

This is one of the ancient Chinese holidays, celebrated on the ninth day of the ninth month (by Chinese lunar calendar—thus, by the Christian calendar, its precise day varies year to year). People went up into the hills to escape epidemics and to visit graves of the ancestors.

By mentioning battlefields, Mao links tradition with his armed struggle.

It was Mao's custom to while away time riding on horseback by humming new poems, which he would then write down later. This was one of them.

DOUBLE NINTH FESTIVAL
October 1929

Easy for human life to age, hard for heaven:
Year after year festival of the Double Ninth.
Now the Double Ninth again.
Battlefields fragrant with yellow flowers.

Year after year the autumn wind is harsh,
not like the spring,
but better than the spring:
endless river and sky,
many thousand miles of frost.

New Year's Day
January 1930

Ninghua, Ch'ingliu, and Kueihua are counties in western Fukien Province in southeastern China where Mao and his German-educated general Chu Teh conducted guerrilla warfare in 1930 on the principles he had set down in rime for that sort of fighting. It is typical of Mao that when he came to phrase military advice in the tersest way, he chose to put revolutionary terms into classical riming form. A crude translation goes like this:

> Enemy advance, we run away.
> Enemy stop, we delay.
> Enemy tired, we annoy.
> Enemy retreat, we destroy.

Mao commented on these lines: "In the past three years the strategy we have learned from our struggle is different from any strategy in history in China and the West. With our strategy, the mass struggle has been spread more and more and more widely; no powerful enemy can stop us. Our strategy is the guerrilla strategy."

The Red Army was moving from Nationalist encirclement through the three counties to conduct the struggle in Kiangsi. They had to pass Wuyi Mountain in Fukien, a place famous for the excellence of its tea.

Given the imminent violence behind the poem, it is charming to consider that the *tzu* which gave it its form is called *Like a Dream*.

NEW YEAR'S DAY
January 1930

Ninghua, Ch'ingliu, Kueihua:
Roads narrow, woods deep, moss slippery.
Where are we going today?
Straight ahead to Wuyi Mountain.
Here under the mountain,
there under the mountain,
the wind blows red flags
like a painting.

On the Way to Kwangchang

February 1930

Kwangchang lies along the eastern border of Kiangsi Province, near the province of Fukien. It was in the area of intense fighting in southeast China after the tiny Red Army left Chingkang Mountain in January, 1929; as Robert Payne says in *Mao Tse-tung*, "They still wore their cotton uniforms, they were covered with lice, and their hair fell down to their shoulders, and many of them walked barefoot. Mao was desperately thin with the strain of commanding the mountain outpost. Less than half the soldiers on the march had rifles: it was assumed that the small column would be able to recoup its armaments from the enemy."

For the next three years in Kiangsi, so-called "annihilation campaigns" were thrown by the Nationalists against the Red Army, which was always outgunned and always outnumbered, sometimes as much as ten times. Payne describes the situation clearly:

The Red armies were ragged, underfed, without cannon or airplanes or any heavy equipment, without reserves, and without more than a handful of trained officers. . . . Yet they nearly always succeeded in inflicting heavy defeats on the enemy, and it was by an exhaustive study of these battles that the Red armies were able to defeat the Kuomintang in 1949. . . . From 1934 onward the study of these campaigns became obligatory in the Red Army. In the first four annihilation campaigns the Red Army in Kiangsi was directed by Chu Teh and Mao. Surprisingly often, Mao's contribution to the strategical operations can be detected. Mao is the surgeon, exploring the wound, insisting above everything else on the delicate probing, the discovery of the enemy's weakened nerve, the dangerous point where weakness is balanced by strength: at this point he will order the attack. There follows a cunning interweaving among the enemy columns—as Mao describes his tactics, they have something of the inevitability of a dance—and finally there is the withdrawal to the chosen terminus, which may be within the enemy lines or deep in enemy territory or safely within the territory the Reds have circumscribed for themselves. The theory, as he relates the battles, seems to be pure Mao; the practice, the knowledge of the possible, the way in which forces can be grouped together for maximum effectiveness, seems to come from Chu Teh. Yet they learned from each other, and it is hardly possible to say where one begins and the other ends. When they came to the borders of Kiangsi and Fukien, Mao was almost entirely inexperienced in warfare. There had been the Autumn Harvest Uprising, followed by the minor guerrilla battles at Chingkanshan. None of these was of any great importance. But in Kiangsi, Mao demonstrated that he was a military genius of the first magnitude.

At the beginning there was almost nothing to show for it. There was the famous four-line slogan invented at Chingkanshan, and there was the knowledge that among the hills of southern Kiangsi the enemy might be lured beyond the reach of its supply columns—the slogan "lure enemy deep penetration" was invented by him during this time. He had not yet begun to think out all the consequences of a strategy of "luring." He was still, as he admitted later, contaminated by Li Lisan's theory of "proletarian uprisings in the large urban districts," but it was impossible to correlate this theory with the small vagrant army, consisting mostly of peasants with a sprinkling of Henyang miners, wandering in the winter hills. His mind fought for certainties, and by the use which he made later of his conceptions of the "first engagement" and the "terminus of withdrawal" it is clear that he found his certainties in these two things.

But where should the first engagement take place? Clearly, the guerrilla troops can choose their own terrain. The Red Army was concentrated along the road from Yungfeng to Hsingkuo, with its main concentrations at Kian [central Kiangsi—EDITOR]. Should the guerrillas remain in the towns? There were heated arguments, for Li Lisan had insisted on the primary importance of the towns, but Mao and Chu Teh

[45]

were already planning a withdrawal into the hills between Kian and Kwangchan. . . .

The Kuomintang generals had hoped to annihiliate the Red Army between the Kan and Ju rivers, but they were themselves annihilated. . . . "In this battle," said Mao, "we faced the enemy with poise and ease."

The Kan River flows north through the hilly area of eastern Kiangsi where the many battles of the five "annihi-lation campaigns" took place in 1930–34. The Red Army was initially successful in applying Mao's principles of guerrilla warfare—eluding, luring, slipping between Na-tionalist divisions. The city Payne calls "Kian" is surely "Chian," on the Kan River some distance south of Nan-chang. It was close to the fighting through several of the "encirclement" campaigns.

ON THE WAY TO KWANGCHANG
February 1930

The whole sky white:
marching in snow
makes the troops more eager.
Overhead, mountains;
red flags, whirled by the wind,
go through the great pass.

Going where?
To the Kan River,
blowing with wind and snow.
Yesterday's orders:
Thousands of workers and peasants march on Chian.

From Tingchow to Changsha
July 1930

Changsha, where Mao went to college, was the great goal which the Red Army wanted but could not take and keep. In June, 1930, the troops reached the walls of Changsha but could not break through the city's defenses.

The phrase "soldiers from heaven" was an ancient expression meaning "soldiers from the imperial court" and is used by Mao to suggest that the Red Army now holds the destiny of China, carrying out the new way of heaven's will.

The "endlessly long reins" probably go back to Chung Chun (139–112 B.C.), who boastfully asked the Emperor Han Wu Ti to give him such reins to bind the King of Yueh and bring him back a prisoner.

There is a fable by Chuang-tzu (*circa* 275 B.C.) about a whale which turned into a roc, an immense mythological bird. The whale was over a thousand miles long when it turned into the roc, and when it flew its wings darkened heaven. Splashes from its wings when it flew over the ocean caused waves a thousand miles high. It rode on a whirlwind, which carried it thirty thousand miles high. The whirlwind rose from the sea in June. Once again, Mao is using Chinese mythology for revolutionary purposes. The whale and the roc represent the evil forces opposed to the Red Army, which with its own strength and dedication (the endlessly long reins) will bind them. Already along one bank of the Kan River people have risen up against the Nationalists ("one stretch is already red" along the Kan). Thousands of peasants and workers join the Red Army to help.

General Huang Kung-lueh (1898–1931) commanded a crack division of peasants and miners.

When the "International" is sung, a whirlwind drops *down* from heaven, instead of rising up, to help.

The "thousands" here should be understood as "many."

In the years of the early 1930s, Kiangsi was the center for building "soviets," for the first sustained battles between Communists and Nationalists. Hunan and Hupei were extensions of this struggle, to the west and the northwest of Kiangsi. Once again, Mao is writing a carefully restrained classical poem under conditions of immediate excitement in the midst of battles which would determine the destruction or survival of the Communist party and of Mao himself.

FROM TINGCHOW TO CHANGSHA
July 1930

In June, soldiers from heaven
fight the corrupt and evil,
with endlessly long reins
they will tie up the whale and the roc.
Over on the Kan River,
one stretch is already red.
The out-flanking division
depends on its General, Huang Kung-lueh.

Workers and peasants, marching by thousands,
roll up Kiangsi like a mat,
drive through Hunan and Hupei.
When we sing the International,
    with a sad excitement,
a whirlwind drops from heaven to help us.

Fighting Against the "First Siege"
Spring 1931

This is another of Mao's poems written during the "annihilation" or "encirclement" campaigns which the Nationalists waged against the Red Army in Kiangsi Province in southeast China, where Mao founded his first peasant soviets. It is yet another example of Mao combining ancient Chinese myth with twentieth century political-military struggle.

Chang Hui-tsan was a warlord in adjoining Hunan Province (Mao's birthplace, famous for its pigs and hot peppers). He joined with the forces of Chiang Kai-shek and made the major attack to destroy the Communists, but was, according to Mao, lured into ambush and himself destroyed. Mao claimed 10,000 men captured by the Red Army, along with 6000 rifles and General Chang in smart uniform, knee boots, and insignia of rank. "How much will you demand for my release?" Chang asked. Nothing was asked: he was taken along to watch the destruction of the other Nationalist troops, then tried and executed.

Mention of Puchou Mountain recalls the myth of Kung Kung, of which there are several versions. Mao chose the one in the book *Huai Nan Tzu* by Liu An in the Han Dynasty (178–122 B.C). According to Mao, Kung Kung and Chuan Hsü fought. In anger, Kung Kung beat his head against Puchou Mountain (not a known place), breaking the pillar which held up the sky and tearing its foundation in the earth. Heaven tilted to the northwest, so that moon and stars moved. Earth opened up to the southeast, so that floods of water, dust, and mud rushed into the hole. Kung Kung triumphed.

As often with Mao, an old myth is used to help prove

one of his constant themes: man is able to change nature by power of will. The ancient order (old China) is displaced; the former system, which had held a steady course like the moon and stars, is pushed aside.

The woods blazing red represent the Red Army; "heaven's soldiers" is the old imperial court phrase for the defenders of the emperor. Mao changes it to mean his defenders of the Communist future.

FIGHTING AGAINST THE "FIRST SIEGE"
Spring 1931

Immense woods under frost sky,
all blazing red.
Anger of heaven's soldiers
soared up to heaven.
Fog over Lungkang, a thousand peaks darkened.
All shout with a single voice:
far up ahead we captured Chang Hui-tsan.

Two hundred thousand troops
break into Kiangsi again,
wind and dust rolling half way to heaven.
Millions of workers and peasants aroused,
all struggle with a single heart:
riot of flags around Puchou Mountain.

Fighting Against the "Second Siege"
Summer 1931

The White Cloud Mountain is about 27 miles east of Huichang County in Kiangsi Province. The Red Army was on the mountain, the Nationalist troops were attacking from below. The official interpretation is that the clouds on the tip represent the Red Army and the "uneasy shouting at its foot" represents the Nationalist forces. "Rotten wood and dying trees" symbolize the Nationalist forces. "Flying Generals" are the Red Army zooming down from the mountain on the Nationalists. The reference is to General Li Kuang in the Han Dynasty who moved swiftly against enemies from the north.

In May, 1931, the Red Army defeated Chiang Kai-shek's troops, who had moved across Kiangsi, setting up forts all along their route with the idea of fighting in security, having some two hundred thousand men to oppose Mao's thirty thousand. Once again, the guerrilla tactics of evasion and of striking the weakest point of the enemy triumphed. On May 15, the Red Army attacked Futien in central Kiangsi and destroyed two Nationalist divisions. At once on May 16, the Communists turned east and in fifteen days marched 700 *li* (230 miles), fighting five battles, capturing twenty thousand rifles, and breaking the "Second Siege." They walked from the gray Kan River to the green mountains in Fukien Province to the east. In these battles, ten thousand Nationalist soldiers were killed and thirty thousand were captured.

"Somebody weeping" means Chiang Kai-shek, his army defeated and his strategy of fortifying each point on his advance into Kiangsi proven to be vulnerable.

[54]

FIGHTING AGAINST THE "SECOND SIEGE"
Summer 1931

White Cloud Mountain:
clouds stand on its tip.
White Cloud Mountain:
uneasy shouting at its foot,
all rotten wood and dying trees struggle,
a forest of rifles threatens,
flying Generals zoom out of the sky.

In fifteen days,
seven hundred *li* march,
Kan River, vague, gray,
Fukien Mountains green.
Thousands of troops swept back,
rolled up like mats.
Somebody weeping:
"Fort at every step" strategy:
What good was it?

Tapoti
Summer 1933

Tapoti is a town 17 miles northwest of Juichin in Kiangsi
Province, the main Red base. Tapoti is said to be a colorful
place, with high mounds of red clay and green pine woods.
Rice paddies and farmhouses with gray tile roofs and white
walls add their colors. Willows line the streams. After rain,
there are rainbows in the sky with as many colors as the
landscape.

"Fierce battles that year" probably refers to the fighting
in February, 1929, in which the Red Army lost heavily but
captured hundreds of Nationalist troops and rifles.

The poem repeats one of Mao's favorite situations—a
landscape beautiful in itself, made more attractive by Red
Army victory and the presence of Communist soldiers and
flags, adding their own colors (including blood) to those of
the town and country.

TAPOTI
Summer 1933

Red, orange, yellow, green,
blue, violet, indigo:
Who is dancing with these
rainbow colors in the sky?
Air after rain, slanting sun:
mountains and passes turning blue
in each changing moment.
Fierce battles that year:
bullet holes in village walls.
These mountains so decorated
look even more beautiful today.

Huichang
Summer 1934

Huichang was one of those modest towns in eastern Kiangsi Province not far from the Communist base of Juichin which gained importance only from the presence of the Red Army. Once again, Mao's unshakable confidence in the Communist cause (and his own self-confidence) are lyrically uttered. This is more surprising, for the summer of 1934 was a losing season for the Red Army, as the Nationalists won portions of south and east Kiangsi and menaced Juichin. It was in October that Mao and the First Red Army gave up their bases in southeast China and began walking on what was to become their most extraordinary achievement, the Long March to the west, thence north in a great curve to Yenan the next year. They even carried sewing machines!

The landscape seems more beautiful, greener, richer when the Communists possess it. The "Eastern Sea" is the East China Sea which lies off the coast of Chekiang. Even the troops remain young ("green") in spirit when they march with the Red Army.

Kwantung is the province lying south of Kiangsi and Fukien, the centers for Communist strength. Taiwan lies off the coast of Fukien and Hong Kong joins Kwantung on its south coast.

HUICHANG
Summer 1934

Dawn about to break in the east:
Surprising that you start out so early.
Tramping all over these green mountains,
men never grow old.
Only on this side
is the landscape beautiful.

Outside Huichang walls, high peaks
stretch ridge after ridge to the Eastern Sea.
Fighting men, looking south toward Kwantung,
point where the landscape
is lush green, green lush.

Three Songs of Sixteen Characters
1934–35

These brief verses were apparently written on the Long March. The reference in the first poem to "three feet three inches" is taken, according to Mao, from a folksong:

> The Mountain of Skulls above,
> The Mountain of Treasures below,
> Three feet three inches from the sky.
> A horse must go unsaddled,
> A man must bend his head to pass.

As always with Mao, his poem defies tradition. The Communists, in mountains so high there is only a crack of space between them and the sky, do not slow down, do not unsaddle their horses, do not bend their heads, either to clouds or to men or to nature. Defiance always is the theme as the Red Army carries its wounded on stretchers and triumphs over snow, cold, hunger, enemy troops. Once again, Mao draws on an older Chinese poem and shapes it to his own purpose.

As they went north on the Long March, the Communists crossed several parts of the massive Kunlun range and finally the high Min Mountains, a little group of struggling, suffering and dedicated men and women. So vast were the mountains that they seemed, in their great cliffs and deep valleys, like waves of an ocean upside down. The second poem uses the image of horses to prove that the small Red Army was still undismayed.

The third poem takes the mountain as a symbol of the revolution, which also is powerful, tall, unassailable.

THREE SONGS OF SIXTEEN CHARACTERS
1934–35

I.

Mountain,
fast horses whipped,
never unsaddled,
suddenly looking back:
only three feet three inches
from peak to sky.

II.

Mountain,
a sea overturned,
waters upside-down in great waves:
hosts of horses
still furious with fighting.

III.

Mountain,
piercing the blue sky,
tip unbroken.
Heaven would fall,
if not held up by that peak.

Lou Mountain Pass

February 1935

Lou Mountain Pass is in northern Tsunyi County in Kweichow Province, described as a thousand peaks penetrating the sky, with the pass a thread through the middle. It was also said that one determined soldier could hold its often one-man-wide trail against thousands. The Red Army reached it after walking 190 *li* without food (approximately 63 miles) on February 2, 1935, having fought their way through many engagements in Kweichow during the Long March. The Reds turned back for a conference at the city of Tsunyi, then returned and stormed the pass a second time on February 26, when this poem was written, almost at once after the Nationalist forces were again defeated. The pass is described as having two thatched houses and a stone tablet with the inscription "Lou Mountain Pass" in three characters at its base. It was said that there was a corner every ten paces and a turn every eight.

Once again Mao proved his astonishing poise at being able to write poetry in a fixed classical form almost at once after physically dangerous experience.

LOU MOUNTAIN PASS
February 1935

West wind fierce,
immense sky, wild geese honking,
frosty morning moon.
Frosty morning moon.
Horse hooves clanging,
bugles sobbing.

Tough pass,
long trail, like iron.
Yet with strong steps
we climbed that peak.
Climbed that peak:
green mountains like oceans,
setting sun like blood.

The Long March
October 1935

On October 14, 1934, some ninety thousand Red Army troops under Mao abandoned their soviet in Kiangsi Province, southeastern China, after severe defeats by the Nationalist Army, and began to walk west, women and children and wounded accompanying them. In the first three weeks, twenty-five thousand men died fighting the blockhouses which Chiang Kai-shek's army had put in their way. It was estimated that fifteen battles were fought, with skirmishes every day. In 368 days on the Long March the Red Army walked 235 days in daytime and eighteen days at night. They covered an estimated 6000 to 8000 miles over some of the most difficult landscapes in the world: deserts, snow mountains, swamps, fast rivers in high gorges, under fire almost every day both on the ground and from planes. In Kweichow they fought both local warlords and the Nationalist Army. Five months of the year there are low clouds over Kweichow Province, which protected them from the air, but they still sustained grim losses.

The Long March was a large personal loss for Mao. Three of his children were abandoned to peasants on the way. When an effort was later made to trace them, they could not be found. His wife Ho Tzu-ch'un was advanced in pregnancy. During a bombing she suffered eighteen to twenty wounds and although she survived, the wounds were still painful after the end of the March in Shensi, northwest China. His brother, Mao Tse-t'an, was killed fighting in 1935 on the March. Mao said that the women showed more courage than the men. Hundreds of women began the March; thirty survived.

[64]

The Five Ridges extend through the provinces of Hunan, Kwangtung, Kwangsi, and Kweichow in southeastern China, very high, very rugged.

Wumeng Range is a lofty barrier on the border between Kweichow and Yunnan provinces.

The upper Yangtze River in Yunnan Province is known as Golden Sands River. The Red Army had to cross it,. although it flows deep and swift through huge gorges and peaks rising a mile high. Chiang's army had occupied all crossings and burned the boats. One day a detachment of the Red Army suddenly reversed its direction and marched 85 miles in twenty-four hours. Dressed in Chiang army uniforms it occupied Chou P'ing Fort and disarmed the garrison. Boats had been withdrawn to the opposite bank, but had not been burned as ordered. In the dark, Red soldiers took a village official to the river bank and forced him to call across to the guards on the other bank that Nationalist government troops had arrived and wanted a boat. They were taken across, and all night troops were ferried to the other bank. When the main body of the Red Army arrived, boats were ready. It was by deception of this kind that the Reds survived, as much as by their small, if determined, force.

The crossing of the Tatu River, in the remote and rugged mountains of far western China near Tibet, was the most perilous and most spectacular fight on the whole March. The area was the home of the Lolo people, never conquered by the Chinese, who were persuaded to help the Red Army. Some joined, and some actually reached Shensi at the end of the March. Others acted as guides over the mountains. One Red officer drank the blood of a newly killed chicken with the high chief of the Lolos, thus declaring that whoever broke the terms of the alliance would prove as cowardly as a chicken.

Reaching the fast Tatu River, they found one boat on the south side and managed to get a small group of soldiers across. But it took four hours for a crossing, and the Red Army could not wait. The troops ferried to the north bank began to march west and the main force on the south bank also marched west, 130 miles of trail so narrow men and animals fell off. At night they carried torches, the flames flickering in the vertical valleys. They stopped only for ten-minute breaks with rest and food (and political speeches on the importance of driving themselves to the ultimate moment of strength). Finally they came to Lutingch'iao ("Bridge Made by Lu"), the only place they could cross. If they did not reach the other side of the Tatu River, they would be annihilated.

There was a precedent for the destruction of rebelling troops in the Tatu area. As always, Snow, in *Red Star Over China*, states it clearly:

The crossing of the Tatu River was the most critical single incident of the Long March. Had the Red Army failed there, quite possibly it would have been exterminated. The historic precedent for such a fate already existed. On the banks of the remote Tatu the heroes of the *Three Kingdoms* and many war-riors since then had met defeat, and in these same gorges the last of the T'ai-p'ing rebels, an army of 100,000 led by Prince Shih Ta-k'ai, was in the nineteenth century surrounded and completely destroyed by the Manchu forces under the famous Tseng Kuo-fan. To warlords Liu Hsiang and Liu Wen-hui, his allies in Szechuan, and to his own generals in command of the government pursuit, Generalissimo Chiang now wired an exhor-tation to repeat the history of the T'ai-p'ing.

But the Reds also knew about Shih Ta-k'ai, and that the main cause of his defeat had been a costly delay. Arriving at the banks of the Tatu, Prince Shih had paused for three days to honor the birth of his son—an imperial prince. Those days of rest had given his enemy the chance to concentrate against him, and to make the swift marches in his rear that blocked his line of retreat. Realizing his mistake too late, Prince Shih had tried to break the enemy encirclement, but it was impos-sible to maneuver in the narrow terrain of the defiles, and he was erased from the map.

In the year 1701, iron chains over 300 feet long had been stretched across the river, with boards tied down as a floor. The bridge swayed in wind down the gorge. Many of the planks had been removed. Nationalist troops were dug in on the opposite bank with a machine gun and a regiment. The bridge could easily have been blown up by the defenders, but it had not been; some of the flooring remained in place. Volunteers were called for, selected; pistols and grenades were strapped on their backs. They started across, hand over hand, under the great chains. The first were shot and fell into the river, but a few worked their reckless way to the point where flooring remained. One Red soldier pulled himself up on the boards and with a grenade eliminated the Nationalist post on the north bank. Soldiers there had thrown kerosene on the remaining planks and set them on fire, but too late. Red soldiers put out the flames, found the planks which had been removed, and replaced them, so that in an hour the whole Red Army was crossing the uncrossable Tatu River, on their way into Szechuan. As had happened before on the March, after the Reds attacked the defending Nationalist troops, many fled and some joined them. For the Red troops who had rushed through the red fire of the bridge, it must have seemed that they were now in the land of peace and security, for in the far west of Szechuan Province there were few Nationalist troops. But now landscape became the enemy—2000 miles of walking over seven immense mountain ranges lay ahead. It was June and warm, but when these southern Chinese in cotton clothing climbed the Great Snowy Mountain, over 16,000 feet high (they could stare west into the clashing and glistening-white peaks of Tibet), many of them died from the cold. Two thirds of the transport animals perished in the ascent of Paotung Kang Mountain, where they had to build their own path over deep mud and rocks. Crossing the Great Snowy Mountain, Mao fell sick and had to be carried. Winds were so strong in the afternoon, men could walk only in the morning. At night some were killed by rockhard hailstones.

On July 20, 1935, the Red Army reached the rich Moukung area in northwest Szechuan, where they met the Fourth Front Red Army of forty thousand well-armed troops. The army rested for a month in the safety of numbers and remoteness. In August, Mao drove on across the

Great Grasslands, dense swamps over which rain fell and fog hovered all through August. Only on narrow paths could they travel, for ten days they saw no human habitation, and yet they depended on food from the wild and hostile Mantzu tribe. It was said that one sheep cost one man's life. The leader of the Mantzus, who hated all Chinese, threatened to boil alive anyone who gave them food. Medical supplies gone, the sick were simply left behind. They were attacked with poisoned arrows and the poisoned mud made their legs blister. They ate wheat green, for there was no firewood. Men stepped into mud and disappeared. They had survived battles and the great mountains, and now enough survived the Grasslands to make a column.

Once clear of the grass and mud, they had to fight Mohammedan cavalry on the high plains, while in Kansu Province more Nationalist troops had been assembled. All were defeated. More losses. Yet on October 20, 1935, they joined the soviet armies in Shensi and were at the end of a journey which had almost annihilated them, but which gave Mao a chance to test his military and political principles and to learn more of China than any of the city-based Nationalist leaders knew.

The last snow-covered peak they crossed was Min Mountain. Never again did the Red Army fight in such country.

Mao himself wrote about the Long March, one of the few aspects of his personal life on which he has talked and written readily:

Speaking of the Long March, one may ask, "What is its significance?" We answer that the Long March is the first of its kind in the annals of history, that it is a manifesto, a propaganda force, a seeding-machine. Since Pan Ku divided the heavens from the earth and the Three Sovereigns and Five Emperors reigned, has history ever witnessed a long march such as ours?* For twelve months we were under daily recon-

* In Chinese mythology, Pan Ku was the creator of the world and the first ruler of mankind. The Three Sovereigns and Five Emperors were also legendary rulers of ancient China.

naissance and bombing from the skies by scores of planes, while on land we were encircled and pursued, obstructed and intercepted by a huge force of several hundred thousand men, and we encountered untold difficulties and dangers on the way; yet by using our two legs we swept across a distance of more than twenty-five thousand *li* [one *li* is approximately a third of a mile] through the length and breadth of eleven provinces. Let us ask, has history ever known a long march to equal ours? . . . The Long March is also a propaganda force. It has announced to some two hundred million people in eleven provinces that the road of the Red Army is their only road to liberation.

The Long March ended at Yenan, a small city of Shensi Province in northwest China, where they lived in caves cut out of the loess ("wind-blown") clay.

Of all the turbulent events through which Mao lived, only the Long March moved him equally to eloquence in prose and intensity in poetry.

THE LONG MARCH
October 1935

The Red Army does not fear
the Long March toughness.
Thousands of rivers, hundreds of mountains, easy.
The Five Ridges
merely little ripples.
Immense Wu Meng Mountain—
merely a mound of earth.
Warm are the cloudy cliffs
beaten by Gold Sand River.
Cold are the iron chains
bridging Tatu River.
Joy over Min Mountain,
thousand miles of snow:
when the army crossed,
every face smiled.

Kunlun

October 1935

Kunlun is the greatest mountain range in China, almost 20,000 feet high, along the border of Tibet and Sinkiang Province in the far west, extending to the interior provinces of the country. An ancient T'ang Dynasty (618–907 A.D.) book said that the shape of the earth had its origin in Kunlun, which runs out in all four directions. It was the place where sacred things grew and the gods lived. The ancient Chinese poet, Chu Yuan (340?–278 B.C.), wrote these lines about it:

> Harness winged dragons for my horses;
> Let my chariot be fine work in jade and ivory.
> How can I live with men whose hearts are strangers
>   to me?
> I am going a far journey to be away from them.
> I took the way that led towards Kunlun Mountain:
> A long, long road with many turnings in it. . . .

"Three million white jade dragons" means snow on the mountain. The author himself made a note about this, referring to a poet of Sung Dynasty (1023–1031 A.D.), Chang Yuan, as Mao, out of wide literary knowledge, so often did. The earlier poet had written:

> After the three million white jade dragons had fought,
> Cast-off scales and broken armor filled the sky.

There is said to be a legend among the country people of the area that when the monkey who accompanied the

[71]

monk on his way to bring Buddhist texts back from India, in the novel *Journey to the West,* passed through the Kunlun area, the mountains were on fire. With his magical powers, which solved all problems along the way, the monkey took a fan of palm leaves and put out the flames. The mountains then turned white.

The line "men change into fish and turtles" means that floods from the melting snow drown them.

In a poem by Yuan Chi (1210–1263 A.D.) from his book *Poems of My Heart* there are these lines:

His influence—the scorching sun or the torrential
  river—extends over a myriad miles.
His bow hangs in the tree on which the sun rests.
His sword leans against the place where the sky ends.

In his poem, *Fu of the Great Hunt,* the great and greatly drunken poet Li Po (699–762 A.D.) refers to a sword: "Therefore pulling out the sword that leant upon the sky." Over and over again Mao turns the ancient poetry of China to a contemporary relevance.

This poem was written in October, 1935, the month when the Red Army completed its Long March from Kiangsi Province in the southeast to Shenshi in the northwest, that walk unsurpassed in human history for distance, suffering, and deaths.

The first stanza concerns the arrogant mountain which startled the sky with cold in winter and drowned men in the melting summer. The second stanza deals with one of Mao's favorite themes—man must try to change nature and the human world. Man, he implies, actually is able to cut nature (and, in other poems, society) down to size.

It is a tribute to the depth of poetry in Mao, and to his astonishing composure, that he could sit down in a cave carved out of the yellow loess soil of Yenan and compose such a temperate poem. After year long death, the loss of three of his own children, intense suffering while crossing some of the highest mountains, bitter cold and burning heat, fighting most of the way, Mao turned not to political polemic but to the ancient Chinese art of the lyrical poem.

KUNLUN
October 1935

Striking into the sky
out of the earth,
Kunlun, monster mountain,
sees all earth's spring colors.
Three million white jade dragons fly up,
freezing the sky with deep cold.
Melting in the summer
rivers flood all over,
men change into fish and turtles.
Who can judge
your virtues and evils
all these thousands of years?

Now I say to Kunlun:
don't be so high,
don't have so much snow.
Leaning against the sky,
could I draw a sword
and cut you into three pieces?
Give one piece to Europe,
send one piece to America,
return one piece to Asia,
a world in peace,
sharing together your heat and cold.

Liupan Mountain
October 1935

Liupan Mountain, in southern Kansu, was reached toward the end of the Long March. It is so steep that the road circles it six times to reach the top. The Red Army had to break through the Nationalist lines at Liupan Mountain before they could enter Shensi Province and the relative safety of Yenan. Watching the wild geese flying south is, for Mao, a moving act, for they are going over that rugged landscape from which the Red Army had just walked.

The Great Wall runs along the northern edge of Shensi Province. Only those heroes who survived the ordeal of the Long March deserve to reach the Great Wall, which Mao uses here as a symbol of China's past, to establish the link of the Communist cause with Chinese history.

The precise distance covered by Mao and the Red Army is not known, estimated figures being from 6000 to 8000 miles. The course was never a straight line but traveled up and down mountains, north, south, west, east, sometimes circling back over places it had already passed. It is probably accurate to say that no one body of men and women, most of the time under attack, all of the time living a minimal existence, has ever walked so far in a single effort.

The conclusion of the poem is Mao's way of saying that the Red Army now holds "the long rope" in its hands, the immediate power, the great future. When shall it conquer the Japanese ("the gray dragon")?

LIUPAN MOUNTAIN
October 1935

Heaven high, clouds light:
watching wild geese
fly south and disappear.
Only heroes will reach the Great Wall.
Counting up, we have walked twenty thousand *li*.

On the peak of Liupan Mountain
red flags ripple in the west wind.
Today the long rope is in our hands:
when shall we tie up the Gray Dragon?

Snow

February 1936

This is probably Mao's best-known poem. It seems to have been given to his friend Liu Ya-tzu when they met in Chungking in 1945 at the fruitless efforts at reconciliation between the Nationalists and the Communists. It was published in a newspaper, *Ta Kung Pao*.

Here again Mao expresses not only his quick sense of the Chinese landscape but also his belief that, great as some of the earlier leaders of China may have been, they lacked a final triumphant quality which would make China great. They were powerful, but they did not bring fulfillment to Chinese life. Snow alters the landscape, the Communist way will turn it red.

The mountains are those of the high plateaus in Shensi and Shansi provinces in the northwest of China.

Chin Huang was the first emperor of the Chin Dynasty (246–210 B.C.). He built the Great Wall. Han Wu (140–87 B.C.), of the Eastern Han Dynasty, fought the Hun invasion from the north. T'ang Tsung (627–649 A.D.) was politically and militarily powerful at the beginning of the T'ang Dynasty, famous for its poetry. Sung Tsu (960–976) was first emperor of the Sung Dynasty. Genghis Khan (1206–1227) was a Mongol emperor.

These five emperors represent traditional old China in every way. It seems that Mao, consciously or unconsciously, compares himself with these emperors, although he rejects them and feels superior to them.

SNOW
February 1936

Landscape of the north:
hundreds of miles ice-frozen,
thousands of miles snow flying.
Look at the Great Wall,
this side, other side,
only white wilderness.
Up and down the Yellow River,
suddenly deep waves disappear.
Mountains, silver snakes dancing;
plateaus, wax-white elephants running,
trying to be higher than heaven.
Some fine day you will see the land
dressed in red, wrapped with white,
flirting, enchanting.

Rivers and mountains so beautiful
heroes compete
in bowing humbly before them.
Pity Emperors Chin Huang and Han Wu,
not brilliant enough in letters.
Pity Emperors T'ang Tsung and Sung Tsu,
not radiant enough in poetry.
That tough spoiled child of heaven,
Genghis Khan,
only knew how to pull the bow
shooting eagles.
All are gone.
For heroes, now is the time.

The Capture of Nanking by the People's Liberation Army
April 1949

Nanking had several times been the capital of China before Chiang Kai-shek made it the seat of government for the Nationalists.

The decisive year of the civil war between the Communists and the Nationalists was 1949, when Peking ("Northern Capital") was captured by the Red Army in January and Nanking ("Southern Capital") in April. From the small armies Mao had in 1945 at the end of the Japanese war, his forces had grown with astonishing speed, until he could truthfully say, as he does in this poem, that he had a million men able to cross the Yangtze and assault Nanking on the south bank. From that day, April 23, the defeat of such Nationalist troops as remained was certain. Some generals took entire divisions over to the Red Army. Peking, indeed, was surrendered without a direct attack. By this time, the Communists were excellently armed with captured American equipment.

It was characteristic of Mao, that old guerrilla fighter, that when he proclaimed the People's Republic of China the parade which crossed the square in front of the Tien An Men, or "Gate of Heavenly Peace," in Peking contained only captured tanks, cannon, and armored trucks. It was also characteristic of Mao that the display of military might should end with *yang-k'o* (rice sprout song) dancers.

It was also characteristic of Mao that he should write a poem about the capture of Nanking within a few days of its taking. He had written earlier poems about battles, "Chingkang Mountain" in 1928, "From Tingchow to

Changsha" in 1930, and the poems on the first and second sieges of the Red Army by the Nationalists in 1931. Many battles did not move him to verse, but the capture of Nanking obviously represented for him that decisive turning away from the past and toward the future which he imaginatively expresses in the last line as ocean turning into fields of mulberry trees, the vision of a new and creative China which occurs so often in his poems as his greatest single theme.

It was also characteristic of Mao that he should, as frequently in his poems, combine Chinese mythology with Communist action. The last line is apparently based on the story of an immortal woman, Ma-ku, who was young, beautiful, with hands shaped like the claws of a bird. She had three times seen the ocean dry up and turn into fields covered with mulberry trees.

Classical writers in China had centuries ago compared the city of Nanking to a "crouching tiger" and the Chung Mountain east of the city to a "curling dragon."

Hsiang Yü was the leader of a force rebelling against the Chin Dynasty in the third century B.C. Wishing to make a reputation for compassion, he did not kill his enemy Liu Pang after capturing him. Later Liu in turn defeated Hsiang Yü, who committed suicide. Liu then became first emperor of the Han Dynasty. The poem is one more example of Mao putting into verse what he had already uttered in prose. At the end of 1947 he had written to the Red Army: "Make wiping out the enemy's effective strength our main objective; do not make holding or seizing a city or place our main objective . . ." This openly explains in prose what his line about Hsiang Yü symbolizes in poetry.

The line, "The sky, if it had feeling, would also grow old," is from the "Song of the Immortal Bidding Farewell to Han" by the poet Li Ho (791–817 A.D.) in the T'ang Dynasty. A translation of the relevant lines would read, "If god could suffer as we do/God too would grow old."

No poems of Mao written between 1937 and 1948 are available. In that period, Mao was engaged in writing theoretical essays such as "On Contradiction," "On the Coalition Government," and "On the New Democracy," and in fighting the Japanese in northwest China, as well as fending off attacks by the Nationalists on Communist bases. It is interesting to quote the interpretation of this poem, and the event it describes, in basically Marxist terms. The following is taken from a translation by Roswitha Haller of the notes on this poem written by Joachim Schickel for the German translation of 37 *Gedichte* (37 Poems by Mao Tse-tung), *Übersetzt und mit einem politisch-literarischen Essay*. No evidence exists to indicate whether Mao accepts this point of view, which argues that Nanking had been the crucial point for opposing domination from the north. It was in Nanking that the T'ai-p'ing rebels began their effort to overthrow the Manchu Dynasty.

Nanking is the wound which the Chinese have inflicted upon each other; for centuries it has attracted war and every time it has paid for its grandeur with ruin. If the lyrical poets say Nanking they mean transitoriness . . . Already the first verse of Mao stands in contradiction to this, when he has wind and rain break out on the Chung Mountain . . . the melancholy of power, the sadness of triumph are swept away. . . .

The appeal to heaven [In this translation,l "sky."—TRANSLATORS] is not accidental: heaven commands that one man rule, it renews the command that a new ruler take the place of the bad ruler; but heaven gives this command through the people and executes it through the army. China's political science, shaped by the ancient Confucian tradition, always considered an overthrow legal as soon as a ruler or his dynasty had lost their command. To our legal thinking, rebellion and even mere resistance are somewhat uncomfortable; it is considered a juridical "illusion" to think that "a legal way and a legal procedure could be opened up" for the revolution, that it could be tamed constitutionally. This European illusion has always been and remained a Chinese reality. Even a historian like Wolfgange Franke, who was not a Communist and only concerned with the truth, could not help seeing the Confucian principle of legality at work in present day China. "Disappointment and exasperation at the total failure of the Nationalist government spread more and more in China," he writes, "the sympathies turned increasingly towards the Communists . . . because people saw in them a healthy power which was not contaminated by corruption, because they alone were capable of replacing the demoralized, no longer viable, government of the Nationalists. The traditional belief . . . of the change in heaven's command played a vital role in this. The Nationalists had not lived up to the command; now it was given to the Communists. Basically, the Communist takeover was no different from similar situations in the past, as, for example, the overthrow of the Mongolian rule or the foundation of the Ming Dynasty."

In the issue 7/1964 of the illustrated *China in Pictures* one of the paintings reproduced "after the verse of Chairman Mao Tse-tung" shows the crossing of the Yangtze: boat by boat . . . they sail under the wind. . . . The crossing of the stream, which is four kilometres wide—formerly considered impossible by experts and afterwards regarded as one of the most important operations of the century—was carried out like a manoeuvre, of gigantic proportions . . . At dawn the first boats took off by the thousands, in the evening there had literally happened what the verse says: a million soldiers stood on the other side of the river; not a poetically exaggerated number, but the actual strength of this army.

On April 21 they had been given this order: Advance bravely and destroy thoroughly, decisively the Nationalist reactionaries who dare to offer resistance within the boundaries of China. Liberate the people in the entire country. Protect the independence and entirety of China's territory and sovereignty. . . . It is known, among others, from Dedijer's biography of Tito, that to the end of the Forties Stalin regarded as unrealistic an uncompromising policy of the Communist party of China and thus he repeatedly tried to make them support Chiang Kai-shek, as he himself practised. An open innuendo to Stalin's advice even against the southern offensive is found in Kuo Mo-jo's commentary . . . : "Before and after the campaign for the liberation of Nanking, there were well-meaning friends, within and without the country, who said we should be content with separate governments in the North and the South of China and should not provoke the intervention of, in particular, American imperialism." [It is assumed that the outside "friend" meant here was Stalin, always very concerned about the Chinese Communists provoking foreign intervention.—TRANSLATORS]

Verse six tells us why Mao did not accept the certainly well-meant advice, why the enemy, particularly since it was desperate, had to be persecuted. Hsiang Yü, tyrant of the kingdom Ch'u, spared the life of Liu Pang when he could have taken it. So he obtained fame as one who showed mercy, and a little later also his own downfall—by the hand of Liu Pang. Anyone who can lose a land apart from his life must learn from Hsiang Yü, he must not value higher the praise of his own humanity than the people who are entrusted to him.

One of Mao's favorite themes in his poems is the triumph of man over nature, controlling it, as with dams and bridges, for social purposes, even changing the sterile salt water into fertile fields. Thus, the last line symbolizes not only the changing of nature but especially the changing of society, the old Nationalist order being turned into more productive and, by the Communist definition, more "democratic" ways.

THE CAPTURE OF NANKING BY THE PEOPLE'S LIBERATION ARMY
April 1949

Over Chung Mountain, sudden wind, rain rising.
Over the Yangtze, a mighty million army crossing.
The city: tiger crouching. Mountain: dragon curling.
The past surpassed,
Sky turned around, earth turned over,
daring and courage.
All bravery left should drive the enemy,
but not like fame-frantic Hsiang Yü.
The sky, if it had feeling, would also grow old,
but in the human world, it is right
for water to turn into fields of mulberry trees.

Reply to Mr. Liu Ya-tzu
April 1949

Mr. Liu Ya-tzu was a poet, a native of Wuchiang in Kiangsu Province. He was a revolutionary from the end of the Ching Dynasty (1911). After welcoming Mao Tse-tung at the Peking airport in late March, 1949, he wanted to return to his native place. Mao wrote this poem to dissuade him. It is in the same form as Mao's poem on the *Long March*: seven characters in each line with strict tonal patterns, rimes, and paired meters, from the T'ang Dynasty.

The two friends used to drink tea together in Canton in 1925 and 1926 when Mao was urging agricultural reforms. In 1941 Liu sent Mao a poem to Yenan telling him that he could not forget "those Canton tea-talks."

In August, 1945, Chiang sent Mao a telegram, requesting a meeting in Chungking, civil war between the Nationalists and the Communists being imminent. Mao replied: "My humble self is most willing to come to Chungking to discuss peace and national reconstruction with you." It was signed, "Your younger brother." The Americans had guaranteed Mao's safety in Chungking. It was the first time he had flown in an airplane. Chiang and Mao were suspicious of each other.

It was while Mao was in Chungking that Liu wrote him a poem: "Nineteen autumns have gone by since our parting in Canton/ Happy now in Chungking to shake hands again." After praising Mao for his bravery in the past years and comparing him to "life-saving rain," Liu says that Mao is like Kunlun Mountain in stature.

Mao wrote the poem *Snow* during this exchange of poems.

The term "old capital" refers to Peking, which Mao and Liu had left in 1918, thirty-one years before.

In his poem written after meeting Mao in Peking, Liu had praised him for his labor, for revolutionising three thousand years of Chinese history, and for writing "exquisite" poems. He also said that they had shaken hands three times in thirty-three years.

Note that, unlike Kuo Mo-jo, who also exchanged poems with Mao, Liu is not called "Comrade" but "Mr." This indicates that, although revolutionary enough to be invited to the New Political Consultative Conference at Peking in 1949 to discuss the founding of the People's Republic of China, Liu was not a member of the Communist party. Liu came, but apparently preferred returning to his native place to staying in the capital city.

While Mao was attending his conference with Chiang Kai-shek in August, 1945, Liu had written a poem for him. Paraphrased, the poem said: Since we parted in Canton, nineteen autumns have passed. I am happy now to shake hands with you again in Chungking. Your acts of bravery have become an example for us. Workers all over the country will receive what they deserve. The land is being built up as if by life-saving rain. History will "thunder out our colleagues of old" (Chiang?). Sun Yat-sen now finds you a companion; a smile, and you are as high as Kunlun Mountain.

Liu had met Mao at Peking airport on March 25, along with a group of other old supporters of the cause. A feast was held in the Hall of Increasing Longevity at the Summer Palace. The crucial line in Liu's poem to Mao on this occasion stated that Mao was revolutionising "our three thousand year history." This was a conviction of Mao's also, that he was simply continuing the ancient history of China.

The Fuchun River is in Chekiang where a certain Yen Kuang of the Han Dynasty (25–220 A.D.) retired from the Imperial Court in order to give his days to fishing and farming. Mao is subtly saying to Liu that he should not leave Peking for the quiet of his native place, but stay with him and work out the problems of the new government. The fishing is better in shallow Kunming Lake than in Fuchun River—the life of work for China, with its turbulence, is better than the quiet life Liu could have in Chekiang Province (on the coast of central China south of Shanghai).

Always classical poetry and Communist attitudes in Mao.

REPLY TO MR. LIU YA-TZU
Five days after taking Nanking. April 29, 1949

(1926)   Drank tea in Canton,
                  I cannot forget it.

(1948)   Exchanged poems in Chungking,
                  the leaves golden.

(1949)   Back in the old capital after
                  thirty-one years.
                  I read your beautiful lines in
                  the season of falling flowers.
                  Do not let too much sorrow
                  break your heart.
                  Keep the whole world always in your
                  farsighted eyes.
                  Do not say that the waters
                  of Kunming Lake are shallow,
                  for watching fish they are
                  better than Fuchun River.

Reply to Mr. Liu Ya-tzu

October 1950

Mr. Liu Ya-tzu wrote: "On the third of October, while at the evening party in the Hall of the Remembrance of Virtues, when songs and dances were given in a combined performance by the Cultural Work Corps of the Southeastern Nationalities, of Sinkiang, of Yenpien in Kirin Province, and of Inner Mongolia, Chairman Mao requested me to fill in these tzus to commemorate this great occasion of unity."

Mao is saying that the history of China was dark; foreign powers came in and compelled concessions; the five hundred million people of China could not make a single, united country. Then the "Sudden cock crow brought light to the sky" (the Communist triumph) with joy even in remote areas like Sinkiang.

The Chinese tradition was that if a man was sent a dedicatory poem, he was expected to reply in the same form with corresponding rimes. Liu had written about lanterns, shining silver, and nightless skies, brothers and sisters dancing, whirling, singing, "the moon is round."

The dancers were from Sinkiang, the dances Uighur; their importance was to emphasize that all peoples of China were first Chinese, but with their individual minority status recognized.

REPLY TO MR. LIU YA-TZU
October 1950

(Watching the opera on Chinese National Day, 1950, Liu
Ya-tzu composed a poem on the spot. I have written this in
the same rime.)

Long night, dawn far away over China skies.
Hundred years, whirling devils danced.
Five hundred million people
could not stay together.

Sudden cock crow brought light to the sky.
Music from everywhere, even from Sinkiang.
Such excitement of poets
has never been before.

Peitaiho

Summer 1954

Between spring and summer Mao visited Peitaiho, a seaside resort on the Gulf of Chihli, close to the small port of Ch'inhuangto, on the old trade route between the great China plains and Manchuria. As he does frequently in his poems, Mao combines nature, history, and poetry.

Yuyen was an ancient name for Hopei Province. In the third century A.D. the Kingdom of Wei was threatened from Manchuria and it was for this reason that Emperor Wu rode past Peitaiho on his way to defeat the invaders.

"Whirling his whip" may have a suggestion that this was what he did best, but Wu was known as a poet as well as a general under the name of Ts'ao Ts'ao. As in other poems, Mao here is interested in a ruler who achieved both power and poetry. Emperor Wu used his whip perhaps as Genghis Khan shot eagles, implying that Mao has changed the state toward a more serious force on behalf of the people rather than being a ruler who merely uses the whip and the bow.

It is said that Ts'ao Ts'ao (Wu)·rode past the promontory of Chiehshih, now sunk into the sea, on his way to fight the Tartars from the north. The autumn wind blew then, as Mao says it still blows. But the urgent theme that Mao asserted so often in his poetry ends his poem: the wind blows again, but the world has changed, China now has its new system.

Ts'ao Ts'ao, like Mao, founded his own state, the Kingdom of Wei in the period of the Three Kingdoms (220–280 A.D.).

Emperor Wu's poem was called "Going Eastward to

Chiehshih." "Bleak and desolate autumn wind" is a line from his poem. Mao often mentions ancient emperors of China in his poems, especially those who also wrote poetry, for they represent old China in its good and its bad. It seems that, consciously or unconsciously, Mao compares himself with them and thinks that he rules with a power at least equal to theirs, but in a way more effective for the people.

PEITAIHO
Summer 1954

Great rains on Yuyen,
white waves foam sky-high,
off Chin Emperor Island,
fishing boats—
none is seen on that immense water.
Where are they?

Over a thousand years ago
Emperor Wu of Wei Dynasty,
whirling his whip,
here wrote his poem "Going Eastward
   to Chiehshih."
"Bleak and desolate autumn wind" blows again.
But the world has changed.

Swimming
June 1956

Every one of Mao's poems is based on a classical form. It is characteristic of his wide knowledge of the older literature that he should base the tune of this poem on an example from the beautiful works of the T'ang Dynasty (618–907 A.D., the greatest period of lyrical poetry in China)—*Water Song*.

Water has been a constant theme in Mao's life as well as in his verse. He swam in cold rivers as a boy, went to school at Hsianghsiang on the Hsiang River, 15 miles upstream from his native village Shaoshan. In May, 1956, Mao left Peking to inspect south China. At Wuhan, he swam across the Yangtze River (flowing 3200 miles from the Tibetan heights across central China to the sea). The poem was written after the crossing by a poet who believed that swimming was one of man's noblest activities. "Swimming is an exercise of struggling with nature," Mao wrote. "You should go to the river, the ocean, to exercise." He also remarked, "Yangtze is a big river, people say. It is big, but not frightening. Is imperialist America big? We challenged it; nothing happened. So, there are things in this world that are big but not frightening." It was characteristic of Mao's rugged individual manner of thinking that he should say: "When you swim in the river, the currents going against you can train your will and courage to be stronger." He believed that the Yangtze was the best natural swimming pool. So enthusiastic about swimming was Mao that he asked, "There are so many rivers in this country. Could all of them be used for swimming? There are six hundred million people in the country. Could there be three hundred million who will swim?"

In the southern suburbs of Changsha (Long Sands), there is White Sands Well. It never overflows, is never dry, its water is always pure and clear. In summer, people come until after midnight to take its famous water. There is a Hunan folk song (Changsha is in Hunan Province) which sings: "Sand water in Long Sands has no sand."

It is heartening, if not actually alarming, in this age of corrupted water to find a song in the period of the Three Kingdoms (220–230 A.D.) which opposes a change in the government's location on the grounds that good as the fish of the new place might be, they were giving up wonderful water. It refers to the removal of the government from ancient Chienyeh (present Nanking) west to Wuchang on the Yangtze:

> Rather drink the waters of Chienyeh
> Than taste the fish of Wuchang.

This is a great tribute to the water, because Wuchang is famous for its fish. So many millions of Chinese live on the salt waters of its long eastern seacoast or on the banks of its many tremendous rivers. Fish is a dramatic item in Chinese diet.

In his reference to Chu, Mao again refers to his classical learning, for in the time of the Warring States, when China was vile with violence (475–221 B.C.), Wuchang was in the Kingdom of Chu.

Mao is cynical about Confucius (551–479 B.C.), saying simply that everything flows away like the river. For Mao's active life, this is too passive. By swimming across the big river, Mao shows how man can conquer nature—not simply flow with the current but oppose it. The saying of Confucius is to be found in his *Analects*.

Turtle and Snake are names of mountains facing each other on opposite sides of the Yangtze, forcing the turbulent waters into a narrow passage. It is here that the long new bridge crosses.

The barrier is the Yangtze, which once formed a division between north and south, but now under the new regime even the Yangtze unifies.

The dam Mao mentions is to be on the upper Yangtze as it flows through Szechuan. It is characteristic of Mao that he should combine the new dam with classical mythology, proving not only the power of people to change their condition but also the persistence of ancient belief. In Wushan there is a Mountain of the Goddess near the site of the dam. An ancient poem of Sung Yu describes how King Hsiang of Chao (298–264 B.C.) dreamed that he spoke with the Goddess, who told him that when she went out in the morning, mists came; if in the evening, rain came. But man will change all of that, Mao asserts, and the Goddess will be surprised by a lake rising in the wild country: the new China astonishing the old

SWIMMING
June 1956

Just drank Changsha water.
Now eating Wuchang fish.
I swim across the thousands-of-miles long Yangtze,
looking as far as the endless Chu skies,
ignoring wind's blowing and waves' beating:
better than walking slowly
in the quiet courtyard.
Today I am relaxed and free.
Confucius said by the river:
All passing things flow away like the river.

Boats sail with the wind.
Turtle and Snake mountains stay,
while great plans grow.
A bridge flies across north to south,
natural barrier turned into an open road.
High in the gorges a rock dam will rise,
cutting off Wu Mountain's cloud and rain.
A still lake will climb in the tall gorges.
Mountain goddess—
I hope she is still well—
will be startled at a changed world.

Reply to Li Shu-yi
May 1957

Yang in Chinese actually does mean the poplar tree, but it also refers to Mao's first wife, Yang K'ai-hui. (Mao had previously been married as a child by his parents to a young girl with whom he never lived.) Edgar Snow comments: "Yang K'ai-hui came from a wealthy landowning family of Hunan. She was the daughter of Yang Ch'ang-chi, Mao Tse-tung's highly respected teacher at the First Teachers' Training School in Changsha. . . . Mao was a frequent visitor in Yang's home; in Peking he frequently dined with the family. . . . Yang Ch'ang-chi obviously had advanced ideas about women's rights or he would not have provided a higher education for his daughter and permitted her to dine at the table with Mao and himself. Mao influenced Yang K'ai-hui toward radicalism —and marriage to himself, in 1920. She was then twenty-five. When arrested by the Nationalists [at Changsha— EDITOR] in 1930, she refused to repudiate the Communist party, or Mao, as the alternative to death. She was executed in the same year, at Changsha. Yang K'ai-hui bore Mao two sons, Mao An-ching and Mao An-ying."

It is interesting to note that Mao An-ying, born in 1920, was thus only ten years old when he was arrested with his mother in 1930. When he was released, other members of the family hid him. During the Second World War he studied in Russia, returning to China in 1948 to work on a commune in Shansi. He was killed on October 25, 1950, when in command of a division in Korea. Mao An-ching was born in Changsha in 1921 and was hidden by friends when his mother was arrested, then sent to Shanghai and later to Russia, from where he returned as a translator and, it is said, as an engineer.

Liu in Chinese means willow. Both the willow and the poplar are symbols of softness, lightness, fragrance; both are common in south China. This reference is to Liu Chih-hsun, husband of Li Shu-yi, an old friend of Mao, who joined the Communist party in 1923 and served as a member of the Hunan Provincial Council and as secretary-general of the Provincial Peasants' Association. He took part in the Nanchang uprising and died in the battle of Hungwu, Hupeh, 1933. His wife did not have confirmation of his death until 1949 after the Communists took over. In 1957 she wrote Mao a letter with a poem about the death of her husband. Mao replied with this poem.

Wanting to become an immortal, Wu Kang of the Han Dynasty (206 B.C.–219 A.D.) committed a grave error for which he was punished by being ordered to go to the moon (manner of transportation not known) and cut down the great cassia tree, 5000 feet in height, which always grew back before the next stroke of the axe. Cassia wine was a drink of the immortals.

There is a legend that Chang O, wife of a famous archer in the Hsia period (2205–1766 B.C.) who had received the elixir of life, stole the elixir and escaped to the moon, where, as the Moon Princess, she found it intensely lonely.

The phrase "the tiger tamed" refers to the destruction of the Nationalists, an event which brought tears (presumably of joy) to Wu Kang and Chang O on the moon.

As always in Mao's poetry, a personal fact, the execution of his wife, is subordinated to the Chinese experience. What in other poets might have remained a private sorrow, becomes with Mao a public event.

REPLY TO LI SHU-YI
May 1957

I lost Yang, that tough poplar,
you lost Liu, that willow—
they flew up to highest heaven.
On the moon, they asked Wu Kang,
What do you have?
Wu Kang brought out cassia wine.

Lonely Moon Princess,
her wide sleeves flowing,
danced in immense space
for that devoted man, that loyal woman.
Sudden news from earth:
the tiger tamed.
Their tears broke out,
turned into rain.

Farewell to the Plague Spirit
July 1958

The "plague" is schistosomiasis, an endemic disease caused by the infection of a blood fluke, *Schistosoma japonicum*. The host is a tiny snail (Oncomelania) from which the disk-shaped larva of the fluke (cercaria), with a taillike appendage, issue. The fluke is of the class Trematoda. Infection was highest in the fertile lands of the middle and lower Yangtze valley, especially in areas adjacent to the big lakes, Taihu, Tungtinhu, and Poyangh, whose tributaries flowed through the most productive land in mainland China. Eleven provinces were affected: Kiangsu, Chekiang, Anhwei, Hunan, Hupeh, Kiangsi, Fukien, Kwangtung, Kwangsi, Szechuan, and Yunnan. The snail flourished in irrigation canals, ditches, rice paddy fields, and slow-flowing rivers. The cercaria infect the body by penetrating the skin of man or animal when it comes into contact in water or wet grass. Eggs of the fluke were diffused by human excrement through its use as fertilizer in fields or the rinsing of chamber pots in watery places. Children playing in water and adults working in the rice paddies were especially vulnerable. The peasants called it "big belly" and believed that unfavorable "wind and water" around ancestral tombs, or evil spirits in the lakes, caused their suffering.

A national survey on the Chinese mainland in 1955 showed that about 10,407,000 people suffered from the disease, and another one hundred million were exposed to infection.* In addition, an estimated 1,500,000 cattle were

---

* Information for these notes is based on an article, "Schistosomiasis in Mainland China," by Tien-hsi Cheng, *The American Journal of*

infected. (It is interesting to note that the disease was also found in such wild animals as the leopard, old world badger, yellow ermine, red fox, lesser Oriental civet, Chinese water deer, wild hog, Rhesus monkey, Himalayan rat, musk shrew, squirrel, south China hare, and a rodent with the distinguished name of Père David's vole—indicating the extraordinary vulnerability of all living things to the wormlike cercaria.)

Most of the endemic areas consisted of rural villages with a mild climate, plentiful water supply, good irrigation, and fertile soils—in brief, where population was dense. Many villages had been desolated and large stretches of fields left idle. Ch'ingpu County near Shanghai, according to Cheng, was once prosperous. In 1955, over half of the 270,000 inhabitants had the disease. Jentun, a village within the county, had about one thousand people before schistosomiasis appeared in 1930. By 1949, only 461 were left, 449 of whom were infected. Eighty of the original 244 families had been destroyed. Houses had tumbled down, and fields were deserted. Of each of twenty-eight other families, not more than one person was living in 1951, at which time 97 percent of the remaining villagers had contracted the disease. According to Cheng, "Equally as tragic was the case of Shangyanpan Village in Yüshan County, Kiangsi Province. The village had a population of over 500 in 1920. By 1949, only 144 survived, including 115 who were languishing with infection. This village was known as the 'Village of Widows,' for schistosomiasis widows were found in almost every household, and many families included widows of three successive generations. In Tzeshih Village of Kiangning County, Hupei Province, the disease levied such a heavy toll on the inhabitants that 12,000 *mou* (mou=1/6 acre) of fertile land which once made the village famous for rice production, were overgrown with weeds. Scourged by famine, the people survived on sea-

Tropical Medicine and Hygiene, Vol. 20, No. 1, 1971, and on invaluable advice from Dr. H. F. Hsü, Department of Preventive Medicine and Environmental Health, University of Iowa College of Medicine.

weeds in spring, wild herbs in summer, husks in autumn, and handouts in winter. Many ended the nightmare of their existence by suicide."

The solution devised by the Communist government of China was typical of the actions of a government whose greatest resource is people. In 1957 a Japanese anti-schistosomiasis delegation had visited China (the disease has all but been wiped out in Japan). Cheng comments:

China has succeeded in doing what is unthinkable in other countries. For instance, an *Oncomelania* snail-extermination campaign was launched in Linhsiang County, Hunan Province [Mao's birthplace—EDITOR], in the winter of 1958 when farm work was at a lull; 30,000 peasants participated. Within two weeks, 20,000 acres of land once abounding with the snail were cleared of this pest and reclaimed for farming. "Human sea" tactics, often effectively employed in major undertakings, enabled China to achieve what seems impossible in western countries.

Depending upon the social and economic conditions of a given locality, different snail-extermination practices are employed. Burying the snail is among the most effective. In China a widely adopted practice of filling in old, snail-infested waterways, ponds, and wells, thereby burying and suffocating the immediate host before installing new irrigation systems, has, in large measure, minimized the hazard of spreading schistosomiasis to newly irrigated areas. On the basis of available reports, the vast expansion of irrigation facilities in mainland China has had little bearing on the spread of the disease; in contrast, in the Congo, Egypt and the Sudan, and Rhodesia, tremendous upsurges of schistosomiasis have occurred after completion of new irrigation projects.

Destruction of schistosome eggs in human and animal feces constitutes an important phase of China's antischistosomiasis campaign since human excreta has been, and still is, the cheapest and most valuable fertilizer available. Formerly, it was a customary practice in the Chinese countryside to store night soil in pits or jars scattered along river banks or near rice fields and to rinse chamber pots in rivers or ditches. Major containers were often flooded by heavy rains, thus causing schistosome eggs to disseminate far and wide.

Under the efforts of the Communist government, the disease has been greatly reduced. In villages, each family deposits its night soil every morning in a large communal container, for which they are paid so many cents a day. The container is sealed when full and left until the ammonia generated has killed the infecting eggs, after which the contents are safe to use as fertilizer. Even fishermen have pots on their boats!

The disease begins with a rash on the skin where the cercaria enters. This is followed by fever, headache, diarrhea, and internal pain in an incubation period of one month during which the worms mature. After that, the symptoms heighten, the disease becomes chronic. There may be a loss of weight, anemia, enlargement of the spleen, cirrhosis of the liver, any of these disabling the sufferer.

The first stanza of Mao's poem deals with the helplessness of the people in the past to control this disease. Hua To was a famous physician of the Three Kingdoms period (220–264 A.D.).

The "cowherd" (a constellation with some stars in Aquila) refers to the Chinese myth that a cowherd lives on a star near the Milky Way. The poet assumes that he meets him in space and the cowherd (by his occupation being interested in rural matters and the health of the peasants) asks him about the plague. Mao makes the sad reply that things are unchanged—there is the same joy, the same sickness.

The second stanza announces the reconstruction of the country, refers to ancient emperors who had worked for the good of China, and dismisses the spirit of the plague by asking where he wants to go—he cannot stay, there is no place for him in the new-built country.

The reference to emperors Yao and Shun is to the same persons mentioned in Mao's poem "Reply to a Friend," Yao giving both his daughters to marry Shun. The two are regarded as models of virtue and as having lived in the remote antiquity of China, in the period 2286–2207 B.C., among the first emperors known. The line means that now all is changed from the dreadful past described in the first stanza, all the six hundred million people of China are, like those ancient emperors, devoted to the general good.

It is likely that by the Five Peaks and the Three Rivers Mao means all of China (the Yellow and the Lo rivers are in north China, the Huai River, running through Anhwei and Kiangsu Provinces, in southeast China). The pickaxes falling and the shaking by iron arms suggest the development of Communist China, the new dams, canals, and other works over the whole country.

The reference to "red rain" may have a contemporary connotation, but probably comes from Li Ho (790–876): "Peach blossoms wildly showering like crimson rain."

Superstitious people would sail paper boats and set them on fire as transports for gods and spirits. Now with the new China, the plague spirit is also being told to go away, as if on paper boats.

The poem is a fascinating example of Mao combining traditional Chinese attitudes and history with the Communist efforts at change. He is implying that in the past people suffered hopelessly, but now, with scientific explorations of problems, the bringing into the countryside of "barefoot doctors," the concern for the peasants, improvements are being made as a natural part of the government's plan.

The immediate occasion for the poem was the announcement in June, 1958, that the disease schistosomiasis had been eliminated in Yukiang County, south of the Yangtze, in Kiangsi Province. This area had special meaning for Mao because he had been with the Red Army during hard fighting against the Nationalists in the late twenties and early thirties in that area. The triumph over the disease was further reassurance of his triumph over the Nationalist forces. No poem of Mao's has a wider variety of influences and references to the Chinese experience, past and present, than this one. Schistosomiasis thus becomes a symbol of Mao's effort to stamp out all that was bad in the past of China.

FAREWELL TO THE PLAGUE SPIRIT
July 1958

Reading in the *People's Daily* of June 30, 1958, about the
stamping out of the blood-fluke epidemic in Yukiang, my
mind became so turbulent I could not sleep. A soft breeze
blew warmly and the rising sun sparkled on the window.
Looking far into the southern sky, I began to write.

— MAO TSE-TUNG

Green water, blue mountain—beautiful in vain.
Even that ancient doctor, Hua To,
could not have stopped these tiny worms.
Hundreds of villages overgrown with weeds.
Sick people shitting.
Thousands of desolate houses—ghosts singing.
Merely sitting here, each day
we travel eighty thousand miles on the turning earth.
Exploring the sky—looking
at a thousand Milky Ways.
The cowherd asked what to do about the Plague Spirit:
the same sorrow and joy still
float on the flowing waves.

Spring wind—willow leaves in thousands.
Six hundred million in China—
all Emperor Yao and Shun.
Red rain of blossoms whirling in waves.

Blue mountains by hard work turned into bridges.
Heaven-touching Five Peaks, pickaxes falling.
Three rivers trembling, iron arms shaking.
May we ask Mr. Plague—where do you want to go?
Paper boats on fire, candles lit, the sky burning.

Return to Shaoshan

June 1959

Mao revisited Shaoshan, his birthplace, after thirty-two years. Note that the poet, unlike many writers going back to the scenes of childhood, does not reminisce about his parents, friends, games, the personal associations of his early years, but about public events and the revolution. It is not his own private emotions but the Communist movement which interests him on seeing again the old village where he had been born in 1893, near the Hsiang River, a tributary of the Yangtze River, which cuts through Hunan Province. The village is south of Changsha.

Mao's father was a moderately well-to-do peasant and dealer in rice, just the sort of man whom Mao came to hate. He did, indeed, intensely dislike and fear his father, who had moments of terrible temper. After one of his father's outbursts, Mao ran away and hid in the woods for three days. When he came back, he had to "kow-tow"—perform the deep bow of submission—to his father.

Mao attended the local primary school until he was thirteen, reading the *Analects* (talks, maxims, aphorisms of Confucius, dating from the fourth century B.C.) and other classics. The teacher is said to have beaten his pupils.

His father expected Mao to work on the farm and to get only enough schooling to help with his accounts. When a teacher urged Mao to attend middle school at Hsiang-hsiang, fifteen miles upriver, his father bitterly opposed it and told him to work on the farm. If Mao had not gone to middle school but had remained a working peasant, it is likely that he might have been a ricebroker all his life and an enemy of the revolution. At the new school he was unknown and disliked.

Edgar Snow, in *Red Star Over China*, states that it was in Shaoshan that Mao heard his first mention of people revolting from some bean merchants returning from Changsha. Snow quotes Mao as having told him:

There had been a severe famine that year, and in Changsha thousands were without food. The starving sent a delegation to the civil governor to beg for relief, but he replied to them haughtily, "Why haven't you food? There is plenty in the city. I always have enough." When the people were told the governor's reply, they became very angry. They held mass meetings and organized a demonstration. They attacked the Manchu yamen [office], cut down the flagpole, the symbol of office, and drove out the governor. Following this, the Commissioner of Internal Affairs, a man named Chang, came out on his horse and told the people that the government would take measures to help them. Chang was evidently sincere in his promise, but the Emperor disliked him and accused him of having intimate connections with "the mob." He was removed. A new governor arrived, and at once ordered the arrest of the leaders of the uprising. Many of them were beheaded and their heads displayed on poles as a warning to future "rebels."

This incident was discussed in my school for many days. It made a deep impression on me. . . . I never forgot it. I felt that there with the rebels were ordinary people like my own family and I deeply resented the injustices of the treatment given them.

Snow also cites another event, a clash between a secret society and a local landlord in which the society withdrew to a mountain called Liu Shan under the leadership of a man named P'ang the Millstone Maker, who was caught and beheaded. Even Mao's own father had some of his rice seized by poor villagers while he was sending it out of the area, which was hungry, to Changsha.

It is an amusing and ironical comment on the Chinese situation that Mao, the greatest confiscator of land in history, had his own land near Shaoshan confiscated by the Kuomintang, the bitter enemy of confiscation. According to Snow, rents paid on that land had been used for the peasant movement in Hunan.

Once more Mao has put into a poem the political texture of his life: no sentimental reveries over childhood, only revolution and the "heroes" who made it.

RETURN TO SHAOSHAN
June 1959

Dream of departure, a curse on vanished rivers.
My native place after thirty-two years.
Red flags woke up the peasant spears.
Black hands held up the tyrant's whip.
Many sacrifices, many strong wills,
will surely change sun and moon
into a new sky.
Happy to see waves after waves of paddy and beans.
Everywhere heroes moving down through the evening
mist.

Ascent of Lu Mountain
July 1959

Lu Mountain is a summer resort in Kiangsi Province.

The "three Wus" are ancient places named Wu along the lower Yangtze River.

The yellow crane has been described in the notes for the poem "Yellow Crane Pavilion."

District Officer Tao Yuan-ming (365–427 A.D.) was a prefect in Kiangsi. He quit his job (it is said, out of distaste for having to bow to others) to be a hermit. In *Peach Blossom Spring* he described an ideal life where people lived in peace and happiness without tyranny or exploitation.

It may be that, in the last lines, Mao is asking whether Tao is aware that the idyllic country he wrote about is actually coming to be in Communist China, but this is less obviously political than most of his poems.

The Chinese literary historian Liu Wu-chi says that Tao ". . . combined in his poems a passion for music and wine, an outlook on life typical of a Taoist recluse, and a sensibility to the delights of nature, particularly its homely and familiar aspects. This earned for him the title 'poet of the garden and field.' "

The text on which Mao bases his reference is an essay of Tao's called "Peach Blossom Spring," which tells about a fisherman who followed a stream until he found a grove of blossoming peach trees:

The fisherman, marveling, passed on to discover where the grove would end. It ended at a spring; and then there came a small hill. In the side of the hill was a small opening which seemed to promise a gleam of light. The fisherman left his boat and entered the opening. It was almost too cramped at first to afford him passage; but when he had taken a few dozen steps he emerged into the open light of day. He faced a spread of level land. . . . Houses stood among rich fields and pleasant ponds all set with mulberry and willow. Linking paths led everywhere, and the fowls and dogs of one farm could be heard from the next. People were coming and going and working in the fields. Both the men and the women dressed in exactly the same manner as people outside; white-haired elders and tufted children alike were cheerful and contented. . . . They told how their forefathers, fleeing from the age of Ch'in, had come with their wives and neighbors to this isolated place, never to leave it. From that time on they had been cut off from the outside world. They asked what age was this: they had never even heard of the Han, let alone its successors, the Wei and Chin. . . .

When Tao retreated from the world, he lived at the foot of Lu Mountain. It is characteristic of Mao to have known this piece of local literary history dealing with the search for a better world, and to have used it in his poem. His use of details from past Chinese culture is, indeed, surprisingly frequent for a man so vigorously involved in the violence of the present time.

ASCENT OF LU MOUNTAIN
July 1959

The mountain, flying, hovers above the Yangtze:
I circle it four hundred times,
running up its greenness.
Cool eyes look over the world beyond the oceans.
Hot winds blow showers of rain
into the sky river.
Clouds cross the nine rivers,
Yellow Crane floating.
Waves roll past the three Wus,
white foam rising.
Where is the official Tao Yuan-ming?
Is he plowing the field by Peach Blossom Spring?

Militia Women
February 1961

The militia was established in 1958, the same year as the communes, to act, if necessary, as an immense guerrilla force spread throughout the country and without a center which could be destroyed. This was the year of the crisis over the offshore islands of Quemoy and Matsu, with the islands bombarded from the mainland and a threat of invasion from Taiwan. There were women on the Long March, as exposed to death and wounds as the men because there was literally no rear area where they could be safe. They were often not only attacked from ahead, but also from behind as the Nationalist troops pursued them. They were, indeed, often surrounded and had to fight their way out, as at Chingkang Mountain. It may be from that experience that Mao decided that women as well as men should be in the militia. The people of the country should be molded into an intense unity, as if 750,000,000 (?) individuals were to act and think and feel as a single person.

MILITIA WOMEN
February 1961
Inscription on a Photograph

Fresh, brave looks—five foot rifles.
First rays of morning light on the drilling ground.
China's girls, alive with highest hope,
they like uniforms, not gay dresses.

Reply to a Friend
1961

Chiuyi Mountain is in Hunan Province. Tungting Lake is north of Changsha; Long Island is the whole area around the lake.

The "Emperor Yao's daughters" reference is to the story that Yao married his two daughters to Shun, who succeeded him as emperor. When Shun died, the daughters wept on his grave by a bamboo grove; forever after there has been "speckled bamboo" in Hunan, its leaves bearing the marks of their tears.

The year 1961 was the decisive conflict of China with the Soviet Union. This poem has a rare sense of Mao yearning toward the province of his youth, its ancient legends, its waters and flowers; and only the last line with its hint of the future ("lit all over with morning sun") has a possibly political implication. It is an uncommonly personal moment in Mao's poetry.

Mao is thinking back to his native province, Hunan, whose lakes are full of lotus flowers.

The four principal rivers of Hunan flow into Tungting Lake, one of China's largest.

REPLY TO A FRIEND
1961

White clouds fly over Chiuyi Mountain.
Riding the wind,
Emperor Yao's daughters come down
through the green mist:
Bamboo speckled with their falling tears,
thousand red clouds, many-layered dresses.
Tungting Lake
foams snow-white to the sky.
Song of the Long Island people
moves the earth:
I want to dream
of traveling through the clouds, looking at the lotus
    land,
lit all over with morning sun.

On a Photo Taken by Comrade Li Chin of the Cave of Immortals on Lu Mountain

September 1961

The cave is on that same Lu Mountain in northern Kiangsi (seat of the first Chinese soviets) about which Mao wrote his poem "Ascent of Lu Mountain" in 1959. The sturdy pines are, like China, undisturbed by the rioting clouds overhead. The cave is a beautiful work of nature. Like the beautiful work of man in shaping a Communist China, the cave exists in the midst of danger.

ON A PHOTO TAKEN BY COMRADE LI CHIN OF THE CAVE OF IMMORTALS ON LU MOUNTAIN

September 1961

Strong pines in the gray glow of twilight,
calm under a whirling chaos of clouds,
Cave of Immortals, creation of nature:
Highest beauty in the dangerous peaks.

Reply to Comrade Kuo Mo-jo

November 1961

However Marxist they became, Chinese Communist leaders kept the ancient tradition of writing poetry. (For centuries in China, qualification for entering government service was based on a literary examination.)

Kuo Mo-jo's poem was called "On Watching *The Monkey Fights the White Bone Spirit Three Times*," which is an opera taken from the classical novel *Journey to the West*. There are surely few examples in history of military and political leaders of a revolution exchanging poems.

Kuo Mo-jo has been one of the leading writers in modern China. In 1921 he helped found the Creation Society, advocating literature for art's sake. By the mid-twenties he turned to proletarian writing in verse, plays, and short stories. He translated from Japanese, English, and German. Kuo also introduced Western images and expressions into Chinese verse. Under the Communists his writing has been reduced to speeches, reports, a few plays, and occasional poetry in a folk song manner. He became vice-premier of the Communist government in 1949, vice-chairman of the Chinese People's Political Consultive Conference, chairman of the All-China Federation of Literary and Art Circles, and president of the Academy of Sciences. He has, in brief, been the party's top literary figure. His poem demands a full knowledge of that astonishingly complex, amusing, and fanciful novel, *Journey to the West*.

Journey to the West deals with the adventures of the Buddhist monk Tripitaka on his way across China to bring Buddhist texts back from India, his many disasters, and his many escapes thanks to his companion, a golden monkey with magical powers. In his admirable book *An Introduction to Chinese Literature*, Liu Wu-chi describes much of the novel's contents: "In the first part are related the birth of Monkey from a magic rock, his coronation as the monkey king, and his attainment of magic powers. The latter include the ability to turn a somersault of 108,000 *li* [36,000 miles]; the mastery of seventy-two kinds of transformation; the use of a mighty iron cudgel which can be changed into a small needle to be placed behind the ear; and the trick of turning his hair, when pulled out, into thousands of little monkeys." There was also a pig on that famous trip; he was notable for stupidity, gluttony, and lechery. There is a wonderful rain-making contest between the local Taoists, in a kingdom they passed through on their way west, and the traveling Buddhist monk and his monkey guardian. The Taoists fail, but when Tripitaka goes to the altar and recites sutras, Monkey points his great iron club and the Old Woman of the Wind appears with a huge bag from which winds rush out and bring such rain that the king begs them to stop.

As with all his use of Chinese myths and history, Mao converts such parts of *Journey to the West* as are most suited to his political purposes. The novel has been interpreted by Marxist-minded critics as showing the oppression by an autocratic society of innocent people and their protection by the folk-hero Monkey. Mao used Kuo Mo-jo's poem as the basis for his own, but he certainly knew the novel well and admired its way of showing how clever intelligence could triumph over dangerous nature as well as evil powers. Kuo's poem reads:

Men and spirits are confused,
so are right and wrong:
Cruel to friends, kind to foes.
Thousands of times the monk chanted the
    Golden Hoop.
Three times the spirit escaped from the
    white bones.
A thousand knives should scrape the monk's flesh.

[119]

Pulling out one hair does not hurt wise Monkey.
Timely teaching earns praise.
Even the Pig is wiser than a foolish man.

Mao's poem is, as usual, imaginative, and yet close to his customary themes. A storm over the earth is always the Communist struggle and its success. The interpretation by Joachim Schickel in his *37 Gedichte* (37 Poems by Mao Tse-tung), *Übersetzt und mit einem politisch-literarischen Essay* (translation by Roswitha Haller from German into English) is curious, fanciful, and heavily Marxist. Schickel asserts that the background for the poem was the historical scene of the moment. The *Peking Review* of April 22, 1960, on the ninetieth anniversary of Lenin's birth, accused the Soviet Union of deviating from real Leninism, citing its willingness to negotiate with the U.S.A. on atomic testing, the visit of Khrushchev to the U.S.A., and the Camp David meeting and preparations for the Paris summit meeting. A film had appeared in Peking based on *Journey to the West* and called "Sun Wu'k'ung's Three Victories over the Spirit of the White Bones," Sun being the Monkey King. Schickel then cites an unnamed source as saying that, "The naive monk can be no other than Khrushchev, while the clever monkey Sun must apparently represent Mao. The monk conjures up destruction, since he refuses to recognize the true nature of the disguised Spirit of the Pale Bones." He then submits that the demon is United States imperialism, but in the end the foolish monk is saved by the great Monkey.

Suspect as so rigid an interpretation may be, there is no doubt that Mao is warning that the threat to the Communist world, although once pushed back, will return.

REPLY TO COMRADE KUO MO·JO
November 1961

Thunder storm abrupt over the earth.
The spirit was born from a heap of white bones.
A monk, if stupid, can be taught,
but a spirit, if evil, must destroy.
Golden Monkey swung his mighty club:
jade sky was cleared of dust
for thousands of miles.
Cheer wise Monkey today,
because that spirit's dust rises again.

Ode to the Plum Tree
December 1961

AGAINST LU YU'S ODE

As he did so often, Mao took an ancient poem and re-versed its meaning while keeping its images to fit the contemporary scene. Lu Yu (1125–1210, the Sung Dynasty) had written:

> Outside the rest house, by the broken bridge,
> lonely, ignored, the plum tree blooms:
> alone, sad in the evening,
> then wind, then rain.
>
> She does not compete for spring—
> let other flowers be jealous.
> Her petals fall, are ground to dust,
> but her fragrance remains.

It is the translators' guess that Mao in his poem means the plum tree to be China. Wind and rain welcomed its arrival, which came out of trouble and difficulty. The tree which blooms while there is still snow is a sign to later flowers. (Communist China is an example for other countries. In Mao's never-diminished optimism, it will "bloom" when the weather is less hostile than when Mao triumphed on the mainland.) In its generosity, China is not jealous of the flowers which will bloom in the warm spring, even though it had to bloom in the snow.

In a note on this poem in his book *Mao and the Chinese Revolution*, Jerome Ch'ên attributes to Kuo Mo-jo the statement that "Ode to the Plum Tree" was first circulated among leaders of the Chinese Communist party during the dispute with the Soviet Union in 1961 to strengthen their morale by pointing out that China had risen above adversity from its beginning.

ODE TO THE PLUM TREE
December 1961

AGAINST LU YU'S ODE

Wind and rain hurried spring's going,
whirling snow welcomes its return:
thousand foot high cliffs, ice-covered,
one flowering twig, beautiful there.

Beautiful, not competing for spring,
only calling that it is coming.
When mountain flowers are in full bloom,
she will be among them smiling.

Winter Clouds

December 1962

Here is another poem in which Mao begins in a traditional Chinese manner with landscape, and then makes his political point in wholly non-propaganda language. This is one more expression of the Sino-Soviet split, with Mao as usual defiantly asserting that China can stand alone against the world, against its weathers, against other countries (tigers and leopards). There is a freezing sky, but in China the earth is warm. "No brave men are frightened by bears" certainly expresses Mao's constant conviction that China does not need Russia. As in his "Ode to the Plum Tree," the plum tree in this poem represents China, which welcomes adversity, knowing it will bloom in spite of it. The flies are the enemies who are so weak that they die in the same weather in which China flourishes.

WINTER CLOUDS
December 1962

Snow weight on winter clouds,
white flakes in flight,
countless flowers falling—
suddenly few.
High heaven whirls with waves of cold.
Great earth gentle with warm air blowing.
Only heroes drive tigers and leopards.
No brave men are frightened by bears.
Plum blossoms like a sky of blowing snow:
Not strange that flies freeze and die.

Reply to Comrade Kuo Mo-jo

January 1963

The poem by Kuo Mo-jo which he sent to Mao stated that six hundred million united people could keep the heavens from falling, that when times are troubled, "heroes" are alert. The whole world hears the cock crowing (the new order) and day breaks in the east. When the sun rises, icebergs melt. Gold resists flames. Four great volumes (the *Selected Works of Mao Tse-tung*) show the way. He writes that it is absurd for Chieh's dog to bark at Yao, meaning that it is stupid for critics to snipe at Mao (this is a reference to an old Chinese saying). Emperor Chieh was a wicked tyrant and Emperor Yao a good ruler. The saying was: "At his master's voice, Chieh's dog barks at Yao." Kuo concludes his poem, that total praise of the new order, by saying that the clay ox plunges into the sea and disappears. (Is the clay ox the Chiang Kai-shek regime on the island of Taiwan?) Revolution, as so often in Mao, is seen as the culmination of Chinese history.

It would seem that "ants on the locust tree" means the external enemies of China who think they can shake that great tree. There is a T'ang Dynasty story by Li Kung-tso about a man dozing under a locust tree. He dreamed that he married the princess of the Great Locust Kingdom and was made prefect of the Southern Branch. When he awoke, he found that the kingdom was an ant's hole under the tree.

The line about mayflies shaking the tree may be taken from a writer, Han Yu (768–824 A.D.), who extended Mao's anti-Buddhist feelings by satirizing an order from Emperor Hsien Tsung to bring a finger bone of Buddha to the capitol. Han Yu said the thing to do was to treat the bone like an honored guest, invite it to dinner, let the dancing girls perform before it, give it gifts, and then escort it to the frontier. It should be treated as you treat any barbarian visitor from abroad. He also argued that it would really be better to destroy it by fire or water. For his boldness, Han Yu was banished to Kwantung province in the south (Canton and Hong Kong are in Kwantung).

Kuo Mo-jo's poem is as follows:

Only when the world's oceans clash in their currents
can heroes prove themselves.
Six hundred million people strong, united,
proud in their principle,
can keep heaven from falling,
can lift up a shattered earth.
Listen: cocks crow all over the world,
day breaks in the east.

Sun rises—
mountain ice melts.
Pure gold will not melt in fire.
Four great books point people the way.
Absurd for Chieh's dog to bark at Yao;
the clay ox dropped into the sea and disappeared.
Revolution unfurls its red flag to the east wind.
The world turns red.

REPLY TO COMRADE KUO MO-JO
January 1963

On this little earth a few flies
hurl themselves against the wall,
humming, humming,
sometimes shrilling,
sometimes weeping,
ants on the locust tree
boasting of being big nations,
mayflies think they can shake the tree.
The west wind scatters leaves over Ch'ang-an,
arrows twanging in flight.

So many human acts,
all of them urgent,
world turning,
time driving.
Ten thousand years—too long!
Seize the hour, seize the day.
Four Oceans storming,
clouds, waters raging;
Five Continents rocking,
thunderstorm roaring.
Sweep away all deadly insects:
No enemy anywhere.

Chingkang Mountain
1965

(See Notes for "Chingkang Mountain," April 1928.)

After thirty years from the time when Mao and the small detachments of the original Red Army were besieged on Chingkang Mountain, hungry, cold, under perpetual pressure from the Nationalist Army, Mao returns to the scene of that early and perilous struggle. Now he is head of the immense country in which the Chingkang Mountain base had been a tiny area, largely unknown. Now there is a monument to celebrate the original occupation of the mountain. As so often, Mao takes the very long view of history—the thirty years elapsed are simply "a moment's snap of the thumb." Nothing is now impossible, the last stanza says, if, like Mao and the leaders who were with him at the beginning, "you can keep climbing." The poem looks to the long future as well as the brief past of the Communist party's control of China.

It is ironical that, in the early Chingkang Mountain poem, Mao talked only of battle. In this later poem, he is relaxed and jovial; he and the others come to Chingkang Mountain this time not with slogans of guerrilla war but with talk and laughter. As always, Mao has an eye for natural beauty and seems deeply pleased that now they come in peace instead of, as on the first occasion, war.

Mao came to Chingkang the first time after repeated defeats, and he left it because he was faced with defeat. For these reasons, coming back was more than an expression of triumph; it was proof that, against an almost total probability that those few revolutionaries of 1927 and

1928 could ever take power in China, the will power to keep climbing could accomplish the apparently impossible.

In August, 1927, the Communists had been defeated in an uprising at Nanchang on the Poyang Lake south of the Yangtze River. Mao was then put in charge of "The Autumn Harvest" revolt, intended to join peasants with soldiers to capture Mao's old college town of Changsha, the ultimate aim being land confiscation and possession of the city. Some of the peasants were armed only with spears and swords. Although some of the eastern Hunan towns were taken, the workers of Changsha did not join the revolt as expected. (The histories suggest that the fault lay with advice from Moscow, which tried to stage the Chinese Revolution as if it were Russian workers and not Chinese peasants who could make it.) The operation ended in total failure and heavy losses. Mao himself was captured, but escaped. When the militiamen who had released him came looking for him again, according to Jerome Ch'ên in his book *Mao and the Chinese Revolution,* Mao hid in tall reeds at the edge of a pond. Next day he collected such remnants of his own Red troops as he could find and fled to Chingkang Mountain.

The landscape was wild, with narrow gorges, tigers, wolves, boars, deer, and pheasants in the woods. There were five tiny villages organized on the ancient clan system. In the recent years Mao had been reproached by the Central Committee of the Chinese Communist party, he had been criticized for leaning to the right, and the Front Committee which Mao had headed was abolished and replaced by another committee of the army, so that Mao was deprived of such command as he had held.

Thus attacked from within his own party, Mao soon was attacked by the Nationalist Army, which was severely defeated by a combination of an ambush in Chihsiling Pass at Chingkang Mountain by Chu Teh (later to become military head of the Red Army and to accompany Mao on the Long March) and an outflanking action by Mao in the rear of the Nationalist troops. The Red forces were continually under siege and attack until January, 1929, when they broke out to the south. Then began that guerrilla warfare which gave the Red Army initial victories but ended with their abandoning the Kiangsi-Hunan area and beginning the Long March, that great walk which ended in the caves of Yenan to the far northwest and ultimately in the capture of Nanking and the establishment of the Communist party of China in power.

As in all his poems, Mao deals in this one not with recollections of friends who had fought with him at Ching-kang Mountain but with the Communist movement itself, inheriting China's history and then changing it.

The intense importance of Mao's return is that, if it could be said of any one place in the Chinese Communist Revolution, "this is where it all began," it would be Ching-kang Mountain.

This poem does not appear in any of the available books of Mao Tse-tung, nor in any of the translations made by others of his poems. It was discovered by Hua-ling Nieh in an issue of the Chinese-language magazine *Ming Pao*, published in Hong Kong, in 1967. Nieh's new novel is currently being serialized by *Ming Pao*.

CHINGKANG MOUNTAIN
1965

A long-time cherished hope:
to fly through clouds
and once more visit Chingkang Mountain.
Coming a thousand miles
to search for the old place,
all changed by a new look.

Oriole singing, swallow dancing, everywhere,
flowing water bubbling,
tall trees climbing into the sky,
Huangyangchieh's paths, then deadly,
now not even steep.

Wind and thunder were violent,
powerful flags were waving.
Now unshakeable on the earth,
the passing of thirty years
a moment's snap of the thumb.

Now we can pick up the moon
in the nine-leveled sky,
and catch turtles in all five oceans.
Triumphant return with talk and laughter:
nothing difficult in this world
if you can keep climbing.

Rejoice at Reading Chairman Mao's Six Poems

Kuo Mo-jo

May 23 of this year is the twentieth anniversary of the publication of "A Talk on Literature and Art at the Yenan Forum" by Comrade Mao Tse-tung. The talk is a development and systematization of the Marxist point of view on literature and art. It not only opened up vast grounds for the new literature and art of China but also received significant attention from revolutionary literary artists in various countries. This year, various groups have been planning the best way to commemorate this anniversary of great historical meaning. The Chairman has agreed to publish in the May issue of *People's Literature* six poems (*tzus*) which he wrote more than thirty years ago. This, in fact, is a joyous event in literary circles. We can predict how the readers, especially literary workers, will rejoice, and how they will be encouraged, and that a great new climax will be reached in literary activities.

Our Chairman does not write poetry casually, nor does he publish it casually. The six poems being published here, together with the other twenty-one poems published before, we can say arbitrarily, are the poetic history of the revolution. This poetic history is not only recorded in language and words but also is cast out in life and blood. Only this kind of poetry can be called creative, revolutionary literature. In the poems, literature and revolution combine into one, creation and life mingle into one and reveal for us literary workers the deep and conspicuous secrets of the process of literary creation.

Our Chairman has said thus in the "Talk":

"China's revolutionary writers and artists, writers and

artists of promise, must go among the masses; they must, for a long period of time, unreservedly and whole-heartedly go among the masses of workers, peasants and soldiers, go into the heat of the struggle, go to the only source, the broadest and richest source, in order to observe, experience, study and analyse all the different kinds of people, all the classes, all the masses, all the vivid patterns of life and struggle, all the raw materials of literature and art. Only then can they proceed to creative work."*

The Chairman's poems have, in fact, been created in just that way. He has provided for us fine examples of the creative process. Of course, the Chairman has not spent all his efforts in literary creation; he revealed his natural emotions unrestrictedly through some literary creations during his spare time after leading the revolution and construction. As the preface of this "Six Poems" says, they were "completed while humming on horseback." This, on the one hand, expresses the Chairman's humbleness, and on the other hand, properly reveals the essence of the process of literary creation. Let us not lightly overlook the word "hum," because in this word is implied the repeated revision of the poems. Poetry is the most refined form of the art of language. It has to have a high degree of metrics, whether of sad grandeur or of grace. Thus, poetry should be able to be read aloud. Strictly speaking, poetry has to be always completed by "humming." Some poetry is completed by humming in studies, some by humming in the fields, some by humming in the factories . . . and the Chairman's poetry is completed by "humming on horseback."

Look, even though the Chairman is galloping in and out of the rain of shells and forest of guns, even though he is coming in and out of life and death, how "steadfast in his commands" he is, how leisurely, how calm, how optimistic! In front of him, the corrupt and evil enemy seems nothing, temporary difficulties seem nothing; the only thing that exists is the victory of revolution, the liberation of the mass

* *Selected Works of Mao Tse-tung* (abridged). (New York: Harper & Row, 1970), pp. 246–51.

of workers and peasants. How could the Chairman have achieved such a spiritual state? It is because the Chairman has "for a long period of time unreservedly and whole-heartedly" lived "among the masses of workers, peasants and soldiers," lived in the highest "heat of the struggle," and lived in "the only source, the broadest and richest source," and finally has incessantly proceeded to "observe, experience, study and analyse"; thus, he has unrestrictedly revealed his emotions as "creative works," and completed his poems by "humming." These poems, these literary works, possess boundless strength of life. They move people deeply and it is impossible for people not to imprint them in their hearts and minds. So, even though the Chairman has "forgotten all of them," they still live in the hearts of numerous *ganpu* (government officials) and the masses of workers and peasants. Take myself, for example, several of the "Six Poems" I have long ago learned by heart.

The Chairman's poems have been repeatedly struck and forged on the anvil, so that they bear an atmosphere of grandeur and yet have harmonious metres and rhymes; they are incomparably impassioned and masculine and yet easy and intimate. Everybody loves to read them; they are put to music everywhere. However, as a matter of fact, it does not appear that everybody understands them. Allow me to give an example—the poem "Lou Mountain Pass" by the Chairman, after the tune of "Yi Chin-ngo" (Remembering the Chin Lady). Last March, at a poetry conference in Kwangchow, I asked for instructions from some comrades who are poetry workers in Kwangchow. Their interpretations were quite inconsistent. Perhaps I should simply quote the whole poem in the following and similarly ask for instructions from poetry workers in the whole country.

West wind fierce,
immense sky, wild geese honking,
frosty morning moon.
Frosty morning moon:
Horse hooves clanging,
bugles sobbing.

Tough pass,
long trail, like iron.
Yet with strong steps
we climbed that peak.
Climbed that peak:
green mountains like oceans,
setting sun like blood.

Lou Mountain Pass, February 1935
translated by
HUA-LING NIEH AND PAUL ENGLE

The first stanza is about morning, and the second stanza is about evening. I asked the comrades in Kwangchow whether the whole poem is about the events that happened on the same day, or about events on different days. Their answers differed. Some said it's about events on the same day; some said it might not be the same day. From this, it seems all of us bear some of Tao Yuan-ming's attitude— "love to read, but with no care for understanding"—and do not actually understand each of the Chairman's poems.

I have done some studies of the poem "Lou Mountain Pass." At the beginning, I felt that they were events on the same day. Later, I checked through the old and new versions of *Chronicles of Tsun-yi City* and found out that the distance from Tsun-yi City to Lou Mountain Pass is 70 miles and takes exactly one day to travel. It's reasonable for a person to start early from Tsun-yi City and reach Lou Mountain Pass at night. After further consideration, I discovered some problems. During the Long March of the Red Army, the first time they passed by Lou Mountain Pass from Tsun-yi City was in January, 1935. The second time they passed by Lou Mountain Pass, returning to Tsun-yi City, was in February of the same year. The season should be around the end of winter and the beginning of spring. But, why is the first stanza in the poem written about autumn? "West wind," "wild geese honking," "frosty morning," are all scenes and objects of autumn. How do we interpret these? It's not plausible to say that the Chair-

[137]

man wrote his poem with no regard for the seasons. Thus, I knew further that "Lou Mountain Pass" does not describe events that occurred on the same day. The first stanza is about the first period of the Long March of the Red Army, the autumn of 1934; the second stanza is about the time after the Tsun-yi Conference when they continued with the Long March and passed through the Lou Mountain Pass for the first time. With this in mind, the entire poem seemed to have come to light.

"West wind fierce" is not simply the west wind of the physical world, it is also a metaphor hinting at the considerably stronger force of the enemy army supported by imperialism. At such a time, in the long dawning sky, the quarter moon is in the second half of the month; in the air, the returning wild geese flying southwards are honking; on the earth, the Red Army on their Long March. The horse hooves are clanging and the bugles sobbing. The atmosphere has a sad grandeur. However, after the Tsun-yi Conference, in which there was established the correct guidance of Chairman Mao in both the party and Red Army, the Chinese Revolution reached a turning point. The poem "Lou Mountain Pass" is a lively reflection of the revolutionary situations before and after the Tsun-yi Conference. After the Tsun-yi Conference, the Red Army marched on with a hundred times more courage. No matter how many irongate passes lay in front, they were to conquer them bravely and heroically. Obstacles abounded ahead—"green mountains like oceans." Blood-shedding struggles had to go on—"setting sun like blood." But, for all these, there must be a victorious tomorrow!

The above is the interpretation I made for "Lou Mountain Pass." I have not asked the Chairman to his face and do not know if my interpretation is correct, but at the poetry conference in Kwangchow, I was glad that the comrades agreed with my interpretation. Perhaps some people might ask: since morning and evening appear in the same poem, why is it not about the same day? This is no rare example in Chinese poetry. For example, in "Encountering Sorrow" by Chu Yuan there are lines like "In the morning,

I drink the dewdrops of the magnolias; in the evening, I dine on the fallen petals of autumn chrysanthemums," or "In the morning, gather magnolias on the bank; in the evening, collect reeds and weeds on the island." All these mornings and evenings are not limited to the same day.

Thus, even though everybody loves to read the Chairman's poems, people might not understand each of them. The reason for this is that we lack the experience of life which our Chairman has; therefore, it is not easy to measure the objective situation and subjective atmosphere in which our Chairman fermented each of his poems. Owing to such circumstances, the comrades of *People's Literature* editorial board, at the time when they obtained permission from the Chairman to publish his "Six Poems," asked me to write some interpretative articles to help young readers understand the poems. I was pleased to accept this happy duty, but I do not do so only for the young reader comrades but for myself as well. Even though I can recite by heart several of these six poems, I have not done further research into the period and circumstance in which each poem was written; so my understanding is also limited. For better understanding on my own part, I have spent several days, with the help of some comrades, especially the help from the comrades at the Department of Central Government Files, and have prepared a preliminary outline of the circumstances in which the six poems were written. Now, I am writing them out for the use of our comrades, hoping that they can be helpful in understanding the Chairman's writings.

WAR BETWEEN CHIANG AND THE KWANGSI CLIQUE
Autumn 1929

This poem, I think, was written between September and October in 1929. In March of the same year, the Red Fourth Army took Changting, which is what the poem says: "Red flags leap over the River Ting."

At the end of May, the Red Fourth Army occupied Lungyen for the first time. At the beginning of June, guerrillas and the masses of that district entered Lungyen for the second time. On June 19, the Red Fourth Army occupied Lungyen for the third time. In September, they wiped out a whole regiment of the Kuomintang troops under Commander-in-Chief Chang Ching in Changping and Yungfu. On September 21, they took Shanghang at dawn. This is what is depicted in the poem: "running all the way to Lungyen and Shanghang." With the above evidence, we can affirm that this poem was written between September and October.

What was the situation in China at that time? The first and second stanzas of the poem serve as a very good contrast. The first stanza is about the tumultuous battles of the warlords: the mountains and rivers of the motherland—the unbroken Golden Vase—have come to a heap of fragments. A great majority of the people were suffering in deep misery.

What then was the situation of the warlords fighting confused battles against each other? It was quite complicated. There were battles among the old warlords, battles among the new warlords, and battles among the old and new warlords. The blind battles began and ended with the year 1929, which was really "raining on man's world all misery."

However, on a bigger scale and more important in its relationship with others is the battle fought in March and May by the Chiang Clique in Nanking against the Kwangsi Clique controlling Wuhan. The Chiang Clique and the Kwangsi Clique had for a long time contended against each other, fighting for territories. Their temporary union lasted until March of that year, and eventually they began war. Thus, in the poem is the line, "Wind and clouds suddenly change."

What was the purpose for these old and new warlords to fight tumultuous battles against each other? It was nothing more than greed for power and profit, trying to claim themselves as kings and lords over the people's heads. But all these wild thoughts of theirs were only dreams. The story of young man Lu's dream in Hantan is known to all. On his trip in Hantan Lu was complaining about his own poverty to old man Lü. Old man Lü gave him a pillow, saying, "Take a nap and it will make you rich, wealthy, and honorable." The young man Lu did as he was told and eventually had a dream in which he became duke and then prime minister; he enjoyed every possible fortune—wealth, happiness, longevity, riches, glory, and honor. When he woke up from his dream, the millet he was cooking for congee was not yet done. This is what is called "theirs is another Millet Dream in sleep." The warlords did not know then that they were dreaming, but the Chairman has already affirmed that they were dreaming like the young man Lu. Viewed from today, this verdict has really become a case of iron truth!

Contrasting the blind battles of the warlords are the revolutionary actions taken by the Red Fourth Army around the southwest of Fukien for the sake of the peasants. They mended a broken fragment of the beautiful mountains and rivers of our country and stepped up land reform. They took the lands of the landlords and rich farmers and divided them among the landless peasants. "We are busy dividing farm and field" is a very lively description.

DOUBLE NINTH FESTIVAL
October 1929

This poem would have been written at the Double Ninth Festival (September 9 on the lunar calendar) in 1929. That year, the Double Ninth Festival fell on October 11 of the solar calendar. How could we know that it was written in 1929? It is because these six poems by the Chairman are arranged in chronological order (see interpretations of individual poems in this essay). Since this one is second to the poem "War Between Chiang and the Kwangsi Clique," written between September and October in 1929, and comes before the next poem "On the Way to Kwangchang," written in February 1930, it can be affirmed that this poem was written in 1929.

The poem was written for the Double Ninth Festival while watching chrysanthemums, which is self-explanatory in the poem itself. The lines: "Easy for human life to age, hard for nature. Year after year, festival of the Double Ninth. Now festival of the Double Ninth again," could easily have been written by others. But, the line, "Battlefields fragrant with chrysanthemums," is typical of Mao. It was, then, a time of war. Look how calm our Chairman was, with the leisure and inclination to appreciate chrysanthemums. Of course, the words "yellow flowers" (huanghua) could only be wild chrysanthemums and not the various expensive breeds planted in yards and gardens. And yet, our Chairman felt them "particularly fragrant"! Does this not express the optimistic spirit of a great revolutionary? It takes such a personality to write such lines. It's difficult to write such lines because it's difficult to *be* such a personality.

Similarly, the lines "Year after year the autumn wind is harsh, not like the spring, but better than the spring" can be equaled easily by others. However, the line, "endless river and sky, ten thousand miles of frost" cannot be easily equaled by any other person. This line not only expresses the author's manner and bearing, like that of the vast sky and open sea, it also reveals his cultivation of the essence of art and culture. Without such manner and bearing, without such cultivation of art, it is impossible to write such lines in the circumstances of war. The word "frost" (*shang*) used here is very sonorous. It is not the ordinary use of the word frost and snow (*shang-hsüeh*) but a representative word for the sheen of autumn. It is the "frost" used in "frost leaves redder than February flowers." But, "frost leaves" are not limited only to "red leaves," there are yellow leaves too. The sheen of autumn is not limited to frost leaves either, there are various fruits and vast and open scenery with high sky and brisk air. .

Spring is the time for the growth of various living things. It does not only reveal colors of red, purple, youthful green, and tender yellow, but in the water and in the air are also incalculable micro-creatures breeding and growing, invisible to the human eye, thus forming an obscure scene. Our ancestors used to call wine "the season spring." But, autumn is different; for all the frost leaves and fruits, all mixed colors, it is a season of harvest and inward-shrinking. All micro-creatures in the air and water stop growing, revealing scenes of "high sky and clear air," "puddles drained and water lucid." This is the reason for being "not like the spring, but better than the spring." Our Chairman's sensitivity as a poet and his courage as a revolutionary have found perfect and impeccable combination in this poem.

ON THE WAY TO KWANGCHANG
February 1930

Comrades told me that the Red Army was engaged in nine attacks on Chian in 1930. The first attack occurred in February; the second, the beginning of April; the third, the end of April; the fourth, in May; the fifth, in June; the sixth and seventh, between June and July; the eighth, the end of August; the ninth, in September and October. The only time for heavy snow was the first attack in February, the rest of the eight attacks were not the time for snow. Thus, it can be proved that this poem, "On the Way to Kwangchang," was written in February, 1930. With the help of this poem of the Chairman's, a record of the weather is kept and preserved. In February of that year, it snowed heavily around the southwest of Kiangsi Province.

The armies that participated in the first campaign were the Red Fourth Army and the Sixth Army. The Red Army arrived at the west of Kiangsi Province on February 5 and took Yütu, Lingtu, and Yungfeng. They had military contact with the enemy army headed by Tang Yun-shan at Shuinan, a short distance away from the southeast of Chian at ten o'clock in the morning on February 24. Half an hour later, the combat came to an end. They had won tremendous trophies. The enemy was routed. This poem was written during the march and would have been completed before February 24. Yütu and Lingtu are mountainous areas. The line, "over our heads, mountains," seems to denote the mountains in this area. Perhaps, it is the Yunshan (Cloud Mountain) in the northwest of Yütu, 1056 metres above sea level.

This poem is a grand picture of marching in snow. In the wind and snow covering the sky, the red flags flutter and fly. Men and horses are in motion. Mountains tremble.

Ambitious and aspiring painters seem to be able to paint such pictures. But, there is one thing which they seem unable to paint. It is the whirling and rising poetic feeling for our Chairman on horseback.

FROM TINGCHOW TO CHANGSHA
July 1930

This poem seems to have been written in June, 1930, soon after the Nanchang Operation.

On June 22 of the same year, the First Division of the Red Army in Tingchow gave orders to other divisions to start out from the west of Fukien and gather at Huichang. On July 11, the headquarters at Hsingkuo gave orders that the attack should start from Hsingkuo and continue to Changshu. At seven P.M. on July 20, the headquarters gave orders from Yungfeng that they should start from Yungfeng and gather at Mohsieh. This is the major force in the Nanchang Operation, as reported in the poem: "In June, soldiers from heaven fight the corrupt and evil, with endless long reins they will tie up the whale and the roc."

The troops of Comrade Huang Kung-lueh (1898–1931) were the right flank division in the Nanchang Operation. He moved eastwards from his base at the Hunan-Kiangsi border to meet the main force at Yungfeng. Here, I should give a brief account of Comrade Huang Kung-lueh's revolutionary activities. He participated in the Pingkiang Uprising in 1928, and served as the party representative in the Second Regiment of the Fourteenth Division in the Red Fifth Army. In winter, the main force of the Red Fifth Army headed for the Chingkang Mountain. He stayed in Pingkiang to take charge of guerrilla warfare. In the autumn of 1929, the main force of the Red Fifth Army returned to Pingkiang; Huang was promoted to the position of vice-commander of the division. At the beginning of 1930, the Red Third Army was established in the west of Kiangsi; Huang became the Army Commander. In June, the First Regiment of the Red Army was established, and the Third Army was incorporated into the First Regiment of the Red Army. From this simplified account, we can understand what the Chairman has said in the poem: "Over on the Kan River, one stretch is already red. The outflanking division depends on its General, Huang Kung-lueh."

Comrade Huang Kung-lueh achieved imperishable accomplishments in the history of the revolution. Unfortunately, he was sacrificed in the Chian-Tungku area in October 1931. That the Chairman particularly pointed out the name of Comrade Huang Kung-lueh during his lifetime reveals the fact that the Chairman had a high consideration for him. When we read this poem, we cannot help saying out loud in our hearts: heroes who sacrifice for the revolution live forever!

The Red Army in the Nanchang Operation had already reached the Niuhang Station in the suburb of Nanchang at the end of July, but, on July 27, Changsha in Hunan Province had already been taken by the Third Regiment of the Red Army; soon, they withdrew. Then, the First Regiment hurried from Nanchang to Hunan to assist. The two regiments met at Liuyang and established the First Troop of Red Army Workers and Peasants of China, prepared to attack Changsha again. However, the enemy's army was reinforced; they had to retreat from Hunan, turned to Kiangsi, and pushed into Chian. They started further and deeper the Land Reform Revolution in the ten districts along the two banks of the River Kan. This circumstance is what is recalled in the poem: "Workers and peasants, marching in millions, roll up Kiangsi like a mat, drive through Hunan and Hupei."

The lines "When we sing the International, that tragic song, a whirlwind drops from heaven to help us" are concrete images of the flourishing development of the revolution in that year. This is to say that the Red Army led by the Communist party stirred up a great storm of revolution in places like Kiangsi and Hunan, and this came as if from heaven. "That tragic song" is the "International." But why tragic? It is because the song has a sad grandeur. Listen, the song is calling: "O Rise, ye slaves of hunger and cold; rise, ye suffering people of the world!" The Chinese people have stood up. They are stirring gusts and gusts of "whirl-wind" under the guidance of the party and the Chairman.

FIGHTING AGAINST THE "FIRST SIEGE"
Spring 1931

This poem should have been written during the period after the victory of the fighting against the first siege and before the victory of the fighting against the second siege.

The war between the forces of Chiang Kai-shek and the combined force of Feng Yu-hsiang and Yen Shih-shan, broke out in May, 1930. Soon after the war, Chiang Kai-shek named the chairman of the provincial government of Kiangsi, Lu Ti-ping (directly under Tan Yen-kai of the Hunan Clique) as commander-in-chief and the regimental commander, Chang Hui-tsan, as the operation specialist. They combined into a force of a hundred thousand and moved towards the Central Government base at the south-east of Kiangsi to launch their first siege. The assignment of the enemy troops ranged from Chian in Kiangsi Prov-ince to Chienling of Fukien Province; they were divided into eight columns, moving down from north to south. The Red Army at that time did not amount to eighty thousand, gathering at districts like Huangpei, Hsiaopu in Lingtu Dis-trict of Kiangsi Province. The enemy troops under Lo Lin to the west of the River Kan were guarding Chian. Three regiments led by Kung Ping-fan, Chang Hui-tsan, and Tan Tao-yuan moved in to occupy the southeast of Chian, and around districts like Futien, Tungku, Lungkang, and Yuantau at the northwest of Lingtu. The main force of Chang Hui-tsan was in Lungkang, Tan Tao-yuan's at Yuantau. These two regiments combined to form the main force of the siege, about fourteen thousand people. Lungkang was close to the Red Army base, had excellent terrain for fighting, and the people were well-disposed. Therefore, the Red Army gathered their strong forces and launched several attacks on Chang Hui-tsan. The attack started on December 27, 1930, and ended January 1 in the next year. They won two big battles in five days. In the first battle in Lungkang, they wiped out the Chang Hui-tsan regiment and held nine thousand people, including the regimental commander, prisoners. They turned around and attacked Tan Tao-yuan's regiment at Yuantau, wiping half of them out. The rest of the enemy ran away on hearing their approach. The fighting against the first siege had a victorious outcome.

The first stanza of the poem sings about the victory of the fighting against the first siege. The campaign started at the beginning of winter, the time of "Immense woods under frost sky, all blazing red." Of course, the word "red" is not simply red, because, in the air there is a whole sky of red leaves; at the firing front is a whole battlefield of the Red Army. The Red Army whose anger soars up to heaven, and the immense woods which pierce the sky, redden both heaven and earth. What a grand and heroic scene! Has the single voice of thousands of shouting people: "Far up ahead we captured Chang Hui-tsan!" shaken the mountains and dispersed the fog which darkened the thousand peaks of Lungkang? Actually, these shouts have also shaken the world. I was then in Japan. I remember vividly that the Japanese capitalist newspapers reported the campaign in particularly bold type faces. It seemed the sky was tumbling down!

However, Chiang Kai-shek did not give up. After the defeat of his first siege, he waited four months and launched his second siege. This time, the enemy's total force amounted to two hundred thousand. Chiang's right hand man, Ho Ying-chin, was the commander-in-chief who guarded Nanchang. Thus, on May 16, 1931, the fighting against the second siege began and ended victoriously on May 30.

The second stanza of the poem gives an account of the beginning of the fighting against the second siege. The lines "Two hundred thousand troops break into Kiangsi again, wind and dust rolling half way to heaven" depict the fierce attack of the enemy. This reveals that the Chairman never took things lightly before a campaign; instead, he took the most serious account of the threatening situation brought by his enemy. Such is the concrete expression of what the Chairman used to say: "In military strategy, we take difficulties lightly; in military tactics, we take difficulties seriously." Eventually, the Red Army aroused hundreds and thousands of workers and peasants, defeating their enemy with a smaller number of people. That is how they obtained victory in the fighting against the second siege.

The Chairman has used in this poem a classical allusion to Kung-kung who butted his head against the Puchou Mountain, which has significant meaning. Kung-kung, while fighting against Chuan-hsu (a legendary ruler of China, 2513–2435 B.C.), was enraged and butted his head against the Puchou Mountain so that the pillar propping up heaven snapped and the rope tied to the earth broke, causing the sky to slant towards the northwest and the sun and moon and other stars to converge in the northwest, whereas the earth in the southeast sank. Thus, the ocean lies in the southeast. This is to say that Kung-kung had changed the situation of the heaven and earth. The Chairman said: "Kung-kung is the victorious hero." Kung-kung is "not dead." Nobody but Mao has ever said this before. Lu Hsun made use of the story about the Puchou Mountain in "Mending Heaven" collected in Tales Retold. I also made use of the same story in "Rebirth of the Goddess." But, both of us said Kung-kung was dead. Lu Hsun, through an officer under Kung-kung, said: "My Chief, thus, butted his head against the Puchou Mountain, broke the pillar of the sky and the rope of the earth; afterwards, my Chief fell off." Here, "fell off" is dead. What my poem said is:

"The people bumped their heads against the rocky cliff at the foot of the mountain. Thunder cracked and fire sparks rose on all sides. Before long, thunder and lightning; the body of the mountain cracked; the canopy of heaven slanted. Black smoke burst out everywhere. Kung-kung and his followers fell dead at the foot of the mountain."

But, the Chairman said Kung-kung was not dead. I sense that this is a process of knowing a view of the universe. From the point of view of Marxism, Kung-kung's spirit of changing nature, changing the objective world, is not dead. It is still living, living forever, in the hearts of laborers, especially living consciously in the hearts of outstanding Communists.

Lu Hsun's story "Mending Heaven" was written in November, 1922. My poem "Rebirth of the Goddess" was written in November, 1920. Our understanding is a great distance from the Chairman's Marxist view of the universe. Thus, at that time, we still did not realize the latent meaning of man changing nature and the objective world in the myth of Kung-kung. After the Chairman pointed it out, it is as if a torch is lifted high to light up the world of Chinese mythology. This will indicate a clear and correct direction in the studies of myths and legends and ancient history. The significance of this, I think, is no less important than the poem itself. Some comrades think that classical allusions should not be used in poetry; some think that commentary is disgusting and consider it pedantic. Actually, they should not take it so negatively. They should see how classical allusion is used and how a commentary is made. For example, is it not new and precise that the Chairman used this classical allusion and made this commentary in the poem?

"Riot of flags around Puchou Mountain"! The Red Army whose "anger soared up to heaven" defeated an enemy five times their size, turning them into "fallen flowers and spilled water" (lo-hua-liu-shui). As such spirit continued to develop, have they not now changed the whole situation of China? How deep the meaning implied in these seven words is! Therefore, we can say: in poetry, allusions with life force should be used and creative commentaries and interpretations should be added!

FIGHTING AGAINST THE "SECOND SIEGE"
Summer 1931

This poem was written in May, 1931, right after the fighting against the second siege.

Chiang Kai-shek, after the defeat of his first siege, was reluctant to give up. In February, 1931, he gathered an armed force of two hundred thousand with Ho Ying-chin, a man under his direct control, as the commander-in-chief. Thus, he started his second siege. This was given a brief account in the last poem. Being aware of Chang Hui-tsan's and Tan Tau-yuan's defeat due to reckless penetration, he employed the way of "going step by step, making careful steps and fighting carefully." From Chian to Chienling, our enemy again built up an 800 mile long fighting front. The Red Army had a force of thirty thousand. Thus, they had to bring overwhelming force to single points. On May 16, they started an attack on the town of Futien 80 miles southeast of Chian, and with one stroke wiped out the two regiments led by Wang Chin-yu and Kung Ping-fan. Then, they turned east, pushing all the way to the border of Kiangsi and Fukien. "Within fifteen days [May 16–May 30, 1931], we marched for seven hundred miles, fought five battles, and captured more than twenty thousand guns; we broke through the 'siege' with gratifying speed." (*Selected Works of Mao Tse-tung*, Vol. I, p. 213.) The second stanza of the poem is precisely about the situation of the fighting against the second siege.

White Cloud Mountain is situated 80 miles east of Huichang in Kiangsi. According to the description in

Chronicles of Chia-ching District, this mountain "has soaring peaks always covered with white clouds." Here, it touches the border of Fukien, and Wuyi Mountain is in sight. (Tingnan of Kanchow also claims a White Cloud Mountain which touches the border of Kwangtung, but it is not the same White Cloud Mountain described in the poem.) The terrain was moved from the town of Futien 80 miles southeast of Chian to the foot of the White Cloud Mountain 80 miles east of Huichang. It was the time when the campaign was soon reaching its victorious end. The scenery before the eyes was "Kan River, vague, gray, Fukien Mountains green." In the cheers of victory, the Chairman's poetic feeling naturally began to surge up again.

The line "all rotten wood and dying trees struggle" it seems to me, is well written in its choice of "rotten wood and dying trees." This can be interpreted in two respects. On the one hand, it is about motivating all the forces, mobilizing the great masses of workers and peasants "to cut woods as soldiers, and hoist poles for flags." On the other hand, it can be said to describe the defeat and escape of the enemy: "Wind screams and cranes cry, everywhere in the woods and grasses are soldiers." It seems to me that the line allows both implications. Please read the first line of the poem, "White Cloud Mountain: clouds stand on its tip." Here, the cloud is personified, with the same enmity against the same enemy, angered and enraged. Since the white clouds are struggling, the woods and trees should struggle too. Of course, this is tactfully imbued with feelings, heroic and impassioned feelings of the masses of victorious workers and peasants, and also of the Chairman, so that green mountains and white clouds, rotten wood and dying trees, have all taken on a positive momentum.

"Somebody weeping," of course, means the enemy weeping, especially the reactionary chief, Chiang Kai-shek. He should be weeping terribly. The defeat of his first siege was because it was not commanded by officers directly under him; but how could he help not weeping now, since this battle was lost by officers directly under him. The first time, they suffered from defeat because they were not taking "one careful step after the other," but this time, they were taking "one careful step after the other," and yet still suffered defeat. How could he not help weeping. But what is the use of weeping? For thirty years, all facts have proved that they had many more chances to weep! A lot of people escaped to Taiwan and have been drawing their dying breaths under the wings of U.S. imperialism. It seems "the Millet Dream" has not awakened yet. History is iron-faced and unfeeling. Anybody against the tide of history, rebelling against the people, against the motherland, can never escape the last judgment of history.

—*May 12, 1962 published in* **People's Daily**

The Minutes of Kuo's Reply to Chairman Mao's Poem

On October 25, 1961, Mr. Kuo, after seeing the performance of the Shao-hsing provincial opera *The Monkey Fights the White Bone Spirit Three Times,* staged by the Shao-hsing Theatre Troupe of Chekiang, wrote a poem entitled "On Watching *The Monkey Fights the White Bone Spirit Three Times*" for the theatre troupe as a token of appreciation and encouragement.

Mr. Kuo compares the "White Bone Spirit" in the play to imperialism and the monk Tripitaka to the Soviet revisionist chief, Khrushchev. Due to the incomparable rage and extreme disgust towards the Soviet revisionist rebels, he directs the spearhead of struggle towards Tripitaka, hinting at Khrushchev. He praises the Monkey's defense of Tripitaka, conquest of the spirit, and protection of the doctrine. Although he was wronged, his devotion for the monk never wavered. Eventually, he is willing to face his master's disaster and rescues Tripitaka. Here is Mr. Kuo's poem:

Men and spirits are confused,
so are right and wrong:
Cruel to friends, kind to foes.
Thousands of times the monk chanted the Golden
  Hoop.
Three times the spirit escaped from the white bones.
A thousand knives should scrape the monk's flesh.
Pulling out one hair does not hurt wise Monkey.
Timely teaching earns praise.
Even the Pig is wiser than a foolish man.

According to Mr. Kuo's account of the process of writing the previous poem, it runs as follows: "Tripitaka in the opera has reversed the wrong and right in the first part; he takes spirits as human beings and he exercises ruthless punishment on his disciple, one who actually conquers spirits and protects the Buddhist doctrine. He even goes to the extent of saying: a priest should have charity; he is not supposed to beat even the real spirits. He keeps chanting the 'Golden Hoop' so that the Monkey suffers from headache and rolls around all over the stage. Finally, he relentlessly writes the letter of dismissal to cut off their master-disciple relationship and thereby drives the Monkey away. When the Monkey kneels to worship at the last moment, he even turns around to ignore it. Seeing the image of Tripitaka on stage makes people feel disgusted, they feel he should be cut ten thousand times by a thousand knives. I have honestly written about this feeling in my poem. 'A thousand knives should scrape the monk's flesh. Pulling out one hair does not hurt wise Monkey,' is my verdict of the monk who acted so that 'Men and spirits are confused, so are right and wrong:/ Cruel to friends, kind to foes.' "

When Chairman Mao read the poem, he thought otherwise and wrote another poem in reply, which is the poem, "Reply to Comrade Kuo Mo-jo" (November 1961).

Through the characters in the play combined with the current events of the anti-revisionist struggle, Chairman Mao has given an appropriate criticism, in his reply, based completely on the revolutionary viewpoint of class analysis and the double contradiction theory. The reply of Chairman Mao's poem directs its spearhead towards the "spirit" —the White Bone Spirit, which harms and haunts people; as to the monk, he considers him the deceived victim who failed to see the truth for the time being, and who, actually, would be the object to win over. This is the fundamental difference between Chairman Mao's poem and Mr. Kuo's.

Mr. Kuo, after reading the reply of Chairman Mao's poem in Canton (Kwangchow), on January 6, 1962, was greatly inspired. Mr. Kuo said: ". . . It's not proper to give the Monk such a criticism in the play. The Monk in the play has been deceived by the White Bone Spirit and therefore is confused with men and spirits, friends and foes. This is the stupidity committed by the stupid. In the second part of the play, when the deceit of the White Bone Spirit is revealed right then and there, the Monk comes to the realization that he has been deceived. He feels regretful and misses the Monkey. Even though the Monkey has been wronged so much, he knows clearly that his master has been deceived. Thus, finally, he himself goes to face his master's disasters; he wipes out the spirits and demons, and saves the Monk.

"The Monkey's manners and attitudes are honest and straightforward. If he takes black as white, confuses right with wrong, takes foes for friends and friends for foes, he is not only deceived by his enemy, as the Monk is, but also surrenders to his enemy and breathes the same air with his enemy. Then, it would be totally different. A person with the intention of taking black for white, confusing right for wrong, is himself a White Bone Spirit or a transformed monster serving the White Bone Spirit. . . . The reply by the Chairman is based on the essence of the thing itself and deals with the problem analytically on a deeper level. The reply by the Chairman actually corrects my radical point of view towards the Monk."

Thus, Mr. Kuo wrote another poem in reply, using the same rhyme employed in the Chairman's reply:

Depending on the thunder bolt in the clear sky,
The White Bones do not come to a heap.
The blinding mist of the nine heavens and four
    seas is cleared.
For eighty-one times, the great calamity is removed.
The Monk, suffering from torment, knows regret.
The Pig, gathering up his courage, tries to repay a
    drop of water and a grain of sand.
The Monkey's golden pupils and fiery eyes give no
    pardon.
He fears not the Spirit's return for a billion times!

Chairman Mao read this reply and wrote back, saying: "The reply is good, no more 'A thousand knives should scrape the monk's flesh.' It's good to take the policy of United Front toward the Centralists."

(The above quoted from "Reading Chairman Mao's poem on *The Monkey Fights the White Bone Spirit Three Times*," published in the May 21, 1964 *Kwangming Daily*, p. 3.)

Bibliography

BIRCH, CYRIL. *Chinese Communist Literature*. New York: Frederick A. Praeger, 1963.

CHEN, CHANG-FENG. *On the Long March with Chairman Mao*. Peking: Foreign Languages Press, 1959.

CHEN, CHI-TUNG. *The Long March*. Peking: Foreign Languages Press, 1956.

CH'ÊN, JEROME. *Mao and the Chinese Revolution*. London: Oxford University Press, 1965.

DEVILLERS, PHILIPPE. *Mao*. New York: Schocken Books, 1969.

GOLDMAN, MERLE. *Literary Dissent in Communist China*. Cambridge: Harvard University Press, 1967.

MALMQVIST, N. G. "The Poetry of Chairman Mao." *Saturday Review*, 27 Nov. 1971, pp. 29–30.

MAO, TSE-TUNG. "New Poems," translated by Rewi Alley. *Labour Monthly* 39: 120–21, 254, 456–57.

——. "Eighteen Poems," translated by Andrew Boyd. *Chinese Literature* 1958, pp. 3–15.

——. *Nineteen Poems*, translated by Andrew Boyd. Peking: Foreign Languages Press, 1958.

——. *Chairman Mao's Poems with Notes*. 3 vols., notes by Chang Shang-tien. Hong Kong: *Wen-hui Daily News*, 1968.

——. "Chingkangshan Revisited, 1965," translated by Jerome Ch'ên. *China Quarterly* 34: 2–5.

——. *Poèmes*, translated by Ho Ju. Peking: Éditions en Langues Étrangères, 1961.

——. *Poems*, translated by Ho Ju. Paris: Argillet, 1967.

——. *Two Major Poems by Mao Tse-tung*, translations

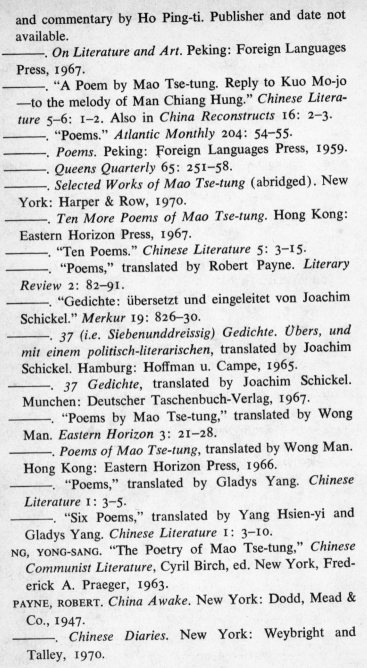

and commentary by Ho Ping-ti. Publisher and date not available.

————. *On Literature and Art*. Peking: Foreign Languages Press, 1967.

————. "A Poem by Mao Tse-tung. Reply to Kuo Mo-jo —to the melody of Man Chiang Hung." *Chinese Literature* 5–6: 1–2. Also in *China Reconstructs* 16: 2–3.

————. "Poems." *Atlantic Monthly* 204: 54–55.

————. *Poems*. Peking: Foreign Languages Press, 1959.

————. *Queens Quarterly* 65: 251–58.

————. *Selected Works of Mao Tse-tung* (abridged). New York: Harper & Row, 1970.

————. *Ten More Poems of Mao Tse-tung*. Hong Kong: Eastern Horizon Press, 1967.

————. "Ten Poems." *Chinese Literature* 5: 3–15.

————. "Poems," translated by Robert Payne. *Literary Review* 2: 82–91.

————. "Gedichte: übersetzt und eingeleitet von Joachim Schickel." *Merkur* 19: 826–30.

————. *37 (i.e. Siebenunddreissig) Gedichte. Übers, und mit einem politisch-literarischen*, translated by Joachim Schickel. Hamburg: Hoffman u. Campe, 1965.

————. *37 Gedichte*, translated by Joachim Schickel. Munchen: Deutscher Taschenbuch-Verlag, 1967.

————. "Poems by Mao Tse-tung," translated by Wong Man. *Eastern Horizon* 3: 21–28.

————. *Poems of Mao Tse-tung*, translated by Wong Man. Hong Kong: Eastern Horizon Press, 1966.

————. "Poems," translated by Gladys Yang. *Chinese Literature* 1: 3–5.

————. "Six Poems," translated by Yang Hsien-yi and Gladys Yang. *Chinese Literature* 1: 3–10.

NG, YONG-SANG. "The Poetry of Mao Tse-tung," *Chinese Communist Literature*, Cyril Birch, ed. New York, Frederick A. Praeger, 1963.

PAYNE, ROBERT. *China Awake*. New York: Dodd, Mead & Co., 1947.

————. *Chinese Diaries*. New York: Weybright and Talley, 1970.

———. *Forever China*. New York: Dodd, Mead & Co., 1945.

———. *Mao Tse-tung*. New York: Henry Schuman, 1950.

SCHRAM, STUART. *Mao Tse-tung*. New York: Simon and Schuster, 1966.

———. "Mao as a Poet," *Problems of Communism*, 13/5, 1964, poems XXI, XXIX–XXXVII.

———. *The Political Thought of Mao Tse-tung*. New York: Frederick A. Praeger, 1963.

SIAO-YU. *Mao Tse-tung and I Were Beggars*. Syracuse, New York: Syracuse University Press, 1959.

SMEDLEY, AGNES. *Battle Hymn of China*. New York: Knopf, 1943.

———. *China Fights Back*. New York: Vanguard Press, 1938.

———. *China's Red Army Marches*. London: Lawrence and Wishart, 1936.

———. *The Great Road*. New York: Monthly Review Press, 1956.

SNOW, EDGAR. *The Battle for Asia*. New York: Random House, 1941.

———. *Red China Today*. New York: Random House, 1970.

———. *Red Star Over China* (paperback). New York: Grove Press, Inc., 1968.

TAY, C. N. "From Snow to Plum Blossom." *Journal of Asian Studies* 25: 287–303.

WALES, NYM. *Inside Red China*. New York: Doubleday, 1939.